Prairie Smoke, a Collection of Lore of the Prairies

Melvin R. Gilmore

Alpha Editions

This edition published in 2024

ISBN 9789361473395

Design and Setting By

Alpha Editions

www.alphaedis.com

Email - info@alphaedis.com

Contents

Prairie Smoke

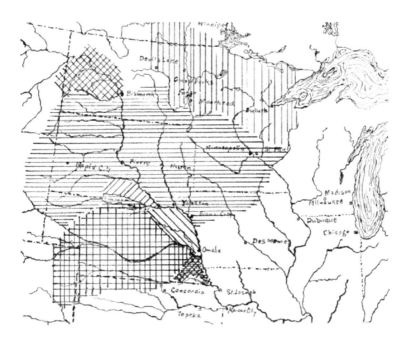

MAP TO SHOW THE DISTRIBUTION OF THE NATIVE TRIBES IN
WHAT IS NOW THE STATE OF NORTH DAKOTA AND
ADJACENT STATES.

The native tribes of North Dakota are of three different linguistic stocks or races. These are the Algonkian, Siouan and Caddoan. The Algonkian race is represented in North Dakota by one nation, the Chippewa or Ojibwa. The Siouan race is represented within our state boundaries by three nations, the Dakota (sometimes called Sioux), the Mandan, and the Hidatsa (who are also called Gros Ventre and Minnetari). The Caddoan race is represented by one nation, the Arikara. Other nations of the Caddoan race are the Pawnees, the Wichita and the Waco farther south.

The domain of the Dakota nation comprised southern Minnesota, northwest Iowa, almost all of South Dakota, part of northwest Nebraska, eastern Wyoming, and the southern part of North Dakota.

The Chippewa domain was around the west end of Lake Superior in northern Wisconsin, northern Minnesota, and part of northeastern North Dakota.

The Mandans, Hidatsas and Arikaras were three nations allied together for mutual protection against the encroachments of their common enemies who pressed upon them from all sides. The Mandan as an independent nation held domain along both sides of the Missouri River in what is now the central part of North Dakota. The Hidatsa were to the east of the Mandan. The Arikara were, some centuries ago, in northern Nebraska, but migrated gradually up the river. Finally they were so pressed by the incursion of the Dakotas from the east that they joined forces with the Mandans, who allowed them place in their country in exchange for the added strength which their numbers gave against the common enemy. The Hidatsas and the Mandans had already, before this, made alliance, so now the three nations were allied in the region of the upper Missouri River within what is now North Dakota, extending westward a little into what is now Montana.

The several domains of the various native tribes or nations within North Dakota and adjacent states are represented on this map as follows:

Dakota by horizontal lines,

Chippewa by vertical lines,

Mandan-Hidatsa-Arikara alliance by oblique cross-hatching,

Ponka by oblique lines slanting to the left,

Omaha by oblique lines slanting to the right,

Pawnee by horizontal and vertical cross-hatching,

Oto by cross-hatching of lines horizontal, oblique left and right.

INTRODUCTION

Many persons are ever seeking outside of themselves and in some distant place or time for interest and cheer. They are always discontented and complaining. They fancy if they were but in some other place or other circumstances they would be happy. But this is a vain fancy. Each of us carries with him the germs of happiness or of unhappiness. Those of unhappy disposition will be unhappy wherever they may be. Cheer is not in environment, but in the individual. One who is of a cheerful, understanding disposition will find interest and cheer wherever he may be.

Robert Louis Stevenson well said "The world is so full of a number of things I think we should all be as happy as kings." When there are so many interesting things in the world, so many in any given place, so many more than one can ever fully know or enjoy in the short span of human lifetime, how can one ever be overtaken by dullness? If dullness seem to enfold us, be sure it is we that are dull; it is because our minds are lazy and our eyes unseeing. There is enough of interest about us wherever we may be to engage our attention if we open our eyes to it. If we have initiative and independence of mind we shall find interest everywhere; but if we depend upon others or neglect what is about us in desire for what is distant we shall never be content. One greater than Robert Louis Stevenson said "The Kingdom of Heaven is within you."

It is with the purpose of calling attention to some of the many fascinatingly interesting things which we have all about us on the prairie plains and in the hills and valleys of our own state, and perhaps in our own neighborhood, that this volume is produced. The myths which pertain to the hills, valleys, springs and streams in our own state and in our own neighborhood must be of interest to us when we look with our own eyes upon the actual places to which these myths pertain. And these myths of the country in which we live are at least equal in beauty and interest to the myths of the Greeks, and to the old Teutonic myths of Thor, Odin, and Freya; or even to our own old British myths which we have from our Druidic ancestors. And however beautiful and interesting in itself a native tree or flower or other plant may be, however engaging to the attention may be a native bird or beast, how much more so when we think of what this bird or beast or flower or tree has been in the lives of generations of our fellow creatures who have lived here and loved this land and its teeming native life long before we ever saw it.

So, it is with the purpose of directing the attentic wealth of lore, of legend and story and myth, and which lies all about us here if we but look and liste is presented.

The title of this book is suggested by one of th flower which is the subject of one of the stori flower, the earliest of all to bloom in springtin prairies, has a number of popular names, among Gosling flower, and Prairie Smoke flower. The la the nebulous appearance presented by a patc blooming upon a prairie hillside in early spring, w still brown and dead. At such a time, with all th the spring wind, they appear to the view like a pu smoke hovering low over the ground.

Besides the reference to this dearly-loved prever smoke" also connotes a number of other eng who has lived upon the prairie this term will both sight and scent. It will recall to the imag billows of smoke which he has seen covering prairie fire; he will see again in memory the showing where some solid particles still smould has passed on leaving behind a vast blackene also the rare, intangible blue haze which for d veil over all the plain, and through which the disk hanging in the sky, while the air was re tang. Again, it brings to mind the wisps o upward in the quiet summer air from stovepi of prairie sodhouses, or which on snowy wint like thin white scarfs against a vast backgroun world.

It will bring to mind also other days and otl country, when there might be seen wreath domes of the hemispherical-shaped hou Pawnees, or Omahas, upon the hills and tilled cornfields and gardens in the fertile all it will recall the scene of an encampment of the prairie on a buffalo hunt in ques encampment is a circle of conical tents, a diameter. Before each tent the evening fir the green of the prairie, a circle of friendly l group, while a few stars begin to twinkle i the sunset colours glow in the horizon.

Some themse title "I

So it is as a " at least destruc

or all of these sights and scents, and others also, will present
lves according to the experience of the one who comprehends the
rairie Smoke."

hoped that to each one who reads this little volume it may indeed be
isp of prairie smoke," and shall bring a real savour of the prairie and
a slight realisation of what the Prairie was before it was swept by the
tive Fires of Change.

DEDICATION

To the Real Pioneers of the Great Plains: to those whose questing spirit
first sought out the wonders and the beauties of this land;—its vast reaches,
league upon league, of grassland, verdant in springtime, sere and red and
brown in autumn; its inviting valleys and its forbidding buttes;—to those
whose moccasined feet made the first human footprints upon the turf of
these prairies and upon the sands of these river margins; whose self-reliance
made them the first to breast the current of these streams; whose humble
footpaths over the land have now become the transcontinental highways of
the world's travel and trade; to those who first slaked thirst at these cool,
clear watersprings, whose hunger was first satisfied by the fruits of this
land, and who, in eating and in drinking, devoutly gave thanks to our tender
Mother Earth for her bounties, receiving them gratefully as sacred gifts to
be prudently used and thankfully enjoyed, and never to be wasted; who
knew and loved this land in all its spacious extent, east to west and south to
north; who reverenced its sacred places, the holy watersprings, the grand
and silent hills, the mysterious caves, the eery precipices,—all places where
their fathers had with prayer and fasting sought and obtained the favour of
the gods, and where the gods had granted revelations and given wisdom to
their fathers; to those whose eyes first beheld this land in its virgin beauty,
fresh and joyous, unscarred and unspoiled, clean and wholesome, animated
with exuberance of life of many species of both plant and animal in
wonderful balance and adjustment, spontaneously replenished; and who
held it a form of sacrilege to violate or in any way endanger the overthrow
of that delicate balance of nature;—to those first inhabitants of this land
which we now inhabit.

That something of their appreciation, of their love and reverence for the
land and its native life, something of their respect for its sacred places and
holy associations; that something of their sense of its charm, of its beauty
and wonder, may come to us; that we may the more worthily occupy and
more sympathetically enjoy our tenure of this land.

To these ends and purposes this book is hopefully and earnestly dedicated.

Land and People

NATURE AND HEALTH

The philosophy of health and wholesomeness of the native Americans, the Indians, was to live in accordance with nature and by coming as much as possible into direct physical contact with the elements in nature, such as the sunshine, the rain and snow, the air and earth. They felt the need and desire to be in frequent and immediate contact with "Mother Earth," to receive upon their persons the strong rays of the sun, the restorative efficacy of the winds from the clean sky, and to bathe daily in living streams.

The priest of a certain ritual of the Pawnee nation visited Washington. He admired the Washington monument as he viewed it from the capitol. When he went over to visit the monument he measured the dimensions of its base by pacing; then he stood up and gazed toward its summit, noting its height. Then he went inside; but when he was asked whether he would walk up the stairway or go on the lift, he said: "I will not go up. White men like to pile up stones, and they may go to the top of them; I will not. I have ascended the mountains made by Tirawa." (Tirawa is the Pawnee name of God.)

Some years ago Mr. Louis J. Hill took a party of people of the Blackfoot tribe to New York City as his guests. They were interested in the sight of the great engineering feats as manifested in the great structures of the city. But they were unwilling to be cooped up in the rooms of the hotel, so they made arrangements to be allowed to set up their tents upon the hotel roof so that they might at least have the natural sunlight and the outdoor air.

In an ancient Pawnee ritual there is a hymn which begins with the words, "Now behold; hither comes the ray of our father Sun; it cometh over all the land, passeth in the lodge, us to touch and give us strength." And in another stanza of this hymn, referring to the passing of the sun, it continues, "Now behold where has passed the ray of our father Sun; around the lodge the ray has passed and left its blessing there, touching us, each one of us."

So it was ever the aim to live in accord with nature, to commune often with nature. A word of admonition from the wisdom lore of the Menomini tribe says, "Look often at the moon and the stars." And the Winnebagoes have a wise saying: "Holy Mother Earth, the trees and all nature, are witnesses of your thoughts and deeds." Another admonition of Winnebago wisdom is: "Reverence the Unseen Forces that are always near you and are always trying to lead you right."

SPIRIT OF LIFE

In the following verses Dr. A. McG. Beede of Fort Yates, North Dakota, has translated a prayer he once heard uttered by an old man of the Dakota nation who had just come from bathing in the river and was standing upon a hill giving expression to his feeling of adoration:

Spirit of Life in things aboveAnd lovelier in things below,We pray to Thee, All-being-love,Spontaneous in our hearts to grow.

Our Father Life, we live in TheeAnd pray for glory which is Thine,And by our living may we beAs Thou art in the Life divine.

The trees and flowers and watersspringsAre singing good old songs of mirth,So may we sing while music bringsThe good old joy o'er all the earth.

Spirit of Life, sing on, sing on;Sing till our aching hearts find restAnd anxious fear is past and gone,And like the rivers we are blest.

The earth is singing, hark the song;The whispering breezes floating by,The waterstreams gliding along,Reflecting faces in the sky.

Spirit of Life, we worship Thee,With waterstreams and trees and flowers;So may our new-born spirits beAs Thou art, and Thy glory ours.

ATTITUDE TOWARDS NATIVE LIFE

People of European race resident in America, (Americans we call ourselves) have sentimental regard toward the plants and animals native to Europe, some of which, domesticated by our ancestors, we have brought with us to America. But most of our people have not developed such sentiments toward the plants and animals native to America. Literary allusions, songs and stories refer to trees, flowers, birds and other forms of life pertaining to our old home lands in Europe, but not to those of America. People of our race have been inhabitants of America now for three centuries, and still we have not made ourselves at home here; we have not formed sentimental attachment to the land and to its native forms of life.

It is a pity for a people not to be so attached to the country in which they live that their sentiments shall be first of all for the forms of life that are native to their own country. Otherwise there is a disharmony which lessens happiness and is harmful in many ways.

Lacking friendly feeling for the plants and animals native to America there has been a tendency to destroy these things in a ruthless manner; and this can hardly be prevented by law unless we can awaken sentimental feelings for the native forms of life in America such as that which our ancestors had for forms of life native in Europe.

Indians, the native Americans, have friendly sentiments, and even feelings of reverence for the forms of life native to America.

I once asked an old Omaha what was the feeling of Indians when they saw the white men wantonly killing buffaloes. As soon as he comprehended my question he dropped his head and was silent for a moment, seeming to be overcome by sadness; and then in a tone as though he were ashamed that such a thing could have been done by human beings, he answered: "It seemed to us a most wicked, awful thing."

Most white men can not comprehend the sense of pain experienced by Indians at seeing the native forms of life in America ruthlessly and wantonly destroyed with no compunction on the part of the destroyers. And this destruction of the forms of native American life by white people gave to Indians a sense of a fearful void in nature, coupled with a feeling of grief, of horror, of distress and pain. It was not fundamentally the thought of the loss of their food supply, but the contemplation of the dislocation of the nice balance of nature, the destruction of world symmetry.

White Horse, an old man of the Omaha tribe in Nebraska, said to me in August, 1913: "When I was a youth the country was beautiful. Along the rivers were belts of timberland, where grew cottonwoods, maples, elms, oaks, hickory and walnut trees, and many other kinds. Also there were various vines and shrubs. And under all these grew many good herbs and beautiful flowering plants. On the prairie was the waving green grass and many other pleasant plants. In both the woodland and the prairie I could see the trails of many kinds of animals and hear the cheerful songs of birds. When I walked abroad I could see many forms of life, beautiful living creatures of many kinds which the Master of Life had placed here; and these were, after their manner walking, flying, leaping, running, feeding, playing all about. Now the face of all the land is changed and sad. The living creatures are gone. I see the land desolate, and I suffer unspeakable sadness. Sometimes I wake in the night and I feel as though I should suffocate from the pressure of this awful feeling of loneliness."

Indians generally were shrewd and discerning observers of the life and habits of plants and animals. The careful study of plants and animals was a considerable part of the courses of study in their system of education, which included much more than is supposed by persons who have not made themselves acquainted with Indian life. They were well informed in plant and animal ecology, and in knowledge of range of species. They took cognizance of the habits of animals in the animals' dwelling places. An old

Indian once told me how a muskrat lays up stores of food in his house. He compared the appearance of the musk-rat's stores to that of a grocer's goods on the shelves of his store. Many old Indians have told me what kinds of food are stored by different species of animals which lay up stores. They often speak of such animals as lay up food stores as being civilized animal nations, and of those which do not make such provision as being uncivilized.

They attribute great wisdom to certain species of animals. This disposition results from discerning observation of the animals' works and ways. The beaver notably is reputed to be very wise and industrious. Indians often sought to gain the favor and learn the wisdom of various animal species by endeavoring to place themselves en rapport with the guardian genius of the species.

INDIANS' APPRECIATION AND LOVE OF THEIR HOMELAND

In the rituals of the various tribes may be found numerous expressions of the love and reverence which the people had for Holy Mother Earth in general and for their own homeland in particular. And in their thought of their homeland they did not regard it as a possession which they owned, but they regarded themselves as possessed by their homeland, their country, and that they owed her love and service and reverence. The following song is found in an ancient ritual of the Pawnee nation which is given entire in the Twenty-second Annual Report of the Bureau of American Ethnology, Part 2. This song plainly reflects the topography and the scenery of the country of the Pawnee nation, that part of the Great Plains traversed by the Solomon, Republican, Platte, Loup, and Niobrara rivers.

SONG TO THE TREES AND STREAMS

I

Dark against the sky yonder distant lineLies before us. Trees we see, long the line of trees,Bending, swaying in the breeze.

II

Bright with flashing light yonder distant lineRuns before us, swiftly runs, swift the river runs,Winding, flowing o'er the land.

III

Hark! O hark! A sound, yonder distant soundComes to greet us, singing comes, soft the river's song,Rippling gently 'neath the trees.

In the foregoing song one can hear the constant murmur of the summer south wind as it blows in that country for days, and see the broad stretch of the great level land, gently undulating in places, with its eastward-flowing streams bordered by zones of trees, the timbered zones along the stream courses being the only forest land in that country.

THRILLING ESCAPE OF A WAR PARTY OUTNUMBERED AND SURROUNDED BY THEIR ENEMIES

A Pawnee Story

In the northwest part of Nebraska there is a high butte with perpendicular sides like the walls of a great building. Because of the shape of this butte, and because it is composed mostly of a soft rock or hard, firm clay, it is called Court-House Rock by the white people. Of course it has other names among the Indian tribes of that region.

This great butte stands out boldly upon the high plain and can be seen for many miles in all directions overlooking the Platte River. The top is almost flat and all sides but one are almost vertical, and are bare of vegetation, worn smooth by rain and by wind, impossible to climb. But there is a way on one side by which a strong man can make his way to the top.

This high lonely butte stands on the borderland between the country of the Pawnees and the country of the Dakotas. The Dakotas and the Pawnees were almost always at war with each other. Many years ago a Pawnee war party was camped near this butte when they were surprised by a war party of Dakotas stronger in numbers than their own party. In the fight which ensued the Pawnees were unable to drive their enemies off, but were compelled to take refuge by climbing to the top of the butte. The Dakotas were unable to follow the Pawnees upon the butte, for the Pawnees were able to guard the single narrow path. But neither could the Pawnees escape again upon the open plain for the Dakotas securely guarded the descent and could easily kill one after another all who might attempt to come down that way. So it seemed only a question of time before all the Pawnees must die of hunger and thirst upon the top of the rock, or come down and give themselves up to death at the hands of their enemies. The camps of the Dakotas surrounded the butte, laying siege to it to starve the Pawnees out.

The Pawnees were in a woeful plight. As the sun rose and traveled across the sky they could look away for miles and perhaps see flocks of antelopes grazing upon the plain, while their own stomachs were pinched with hunger; and some miles to the south they could see the flashing sunlight gleaming upon the waters of the Platte River, while close at hand, at the foot of the butte, they could see their enemies eating and drinking, which could but serve to aggravate their own hunger and thirst. And at night when the scorching sun had sunk in the west they might look away to the eastward, in which direction their homes lay many days' march distant in the beautiful and fruitful valley of the Loup River; and as they looked the twinkling stars appearing one by one near the eastern horizon must have made them think of the evening camp fires of their home people. And at night the grim chill of the rare air of the high butte gripped their bodies in its clutch. And all the while they must be very vigilant against their enemies to prevent being overtaken. They all suffered severely, but the captain of the company suffered most of all; for added to the bodily sufferings which he endured in common with his men, he also suffered extreme mental anguish, for he felt his responsibility on account of his men. Because they had trusted his leadership and had put themselves under his orders it seemed that now they must all die a horrible death. For himself he dreaded not death so much as to be the cause of the loss of his brave men. To him this was far more bitter than death. In the night-time he would go away from the others and cry out in fervent prayer to Tirawa, begging His help, begging that He would show him some way to save his men and bring them off safe.

And while he was thus praying, he heard a voice saying, "Look carefully and see if you can find a place where you shall be able to climb down from this rock and save your men and yourself." So he prayed earnestly all night, and when daylight came he went along the edges of the butte looking carefully to see if there might be a place where some way might be found by which to go down. At last he found a jutting point of rock near the cliff edge, and standing above the level. Below this point the cliff side was smooth and vertical. It occurred to him that this point might be made a means of support from which the men might let themselves down the face of the cliff by a rope. When night came again, after he had posted the sentries to guard the place of ascent from the enemy, he returned to the point of rock and with his knife he cut away soft weathered rock at its base to make a secure place of fastening for a rope. Then he gathered secretly all the lariats which the company had. These he tied together and then, tying one end securely to the rock which he had prepared, he carefully paid out the rope and found to his joy that it reached the ground below. He made a loop in the rope for his foot and then he let himself slowly down to the ground, then he climbed back again. When night came again he posted his sentries so that the enemy might see them at their posts on the side of the butte above the path, but when darkness had fully come they were all gradually withdrawn. Quietly calling his men about him he explained his plan and told them how they might all save themselves. He sent his men down by the rope, one after another, beginning with the youngest and least important of the company, and so on up to the men of most importance. Last of all the captain of the company himself came down. He and all his men crept quietly in the darkness through the Dakota lines and escaped safely. The Dakotas directed their vigilance mainly toward the other side of the butte where lay the only path, and that a very rugged one, between the base and the summit.

The Pawnees never knew how long the Dakotas kept watch about the rock.

A MANDAN MONUMENT IN COMMEMORATION OF AN ACT OF HEROISM

It is a common instinct among all nations of the human race to preserve relics and record memorials of notable persons and events. Such monuments vary with the different means and materials at hand. Sometimes mounds of earth, sometimes boulders, sometimes cairns of stones, sometimes hewn stones, and various other devices have been used according to circumstances.

There exists a monument to the memory of a Mandan hero which has never before been described and published. The following account is from information given by several persons of the Mandan, Hidatsa and Arikara tribes. The location of the monument is near the site of "Fish-hook Village" on the north side of the Missouri River some twelve or fifteen miles east of Elbowoods, North Dakota.

During the middle part of the 19th century the three tribes, Arikara, Hidatsa and Mandan, lived together in alliance against their common enemies. Their chief enemies were the Dakota. So these three tribes built their three villages adjoining, making one compound village of three wards. The village lay upon a well-drained terrace of the Missouri River, while their farms were laid out in the fertile alluvial "bottom" along the river both above and below the village. To the north of the village site lies a range of hills.

The enemy many times made raids upon the village. They would approach under cover of the hills to the north and then steal close upon the village through the course of a ravine which skirted the northeast and north sides of the village.

About sixty-six years ago such an attack was made by a war party of Dakota. Of the defenders of the village, two young Mandans, brothers, named Lefthand and Redleaf, had been dismounted and their retreat cut off by the enemy. A brother of these two, Whitecrow by name, saw the danger of Lefthand and Redleaf and rode out to their assistance. Lefthand was killed and Redleaf was defending the body from a Dakota who was trying to take the scalp. Redleaf shot at the Dakota and missed him, the bullet going over the enemy's head and striking into the ground beyond him, the enemy being crouched low at the time of the shot. Whitecrow rode in a circuit beyond these combatants and held off the attacking party of the enemy. He killed the Dakota who was engaged in combat with his brother Redleaf. Then Whitecrow picked up Redleaf upon the horse with himself and carried him safely back to the village.

After the enemy had been driven away the Mandans went out and marked the course in which Whitecrow had ridden to his brother's rescue, the spot where Lefthand had been killed, the spot where Redleaf had made his stand, the spot where the Dakota was killed, and the spot where Redleaf's bullet fired at the Dakota, had struck the ground. The method used for marking these places was by removal of the sod leaving holes in the ground. To mark the course of Whitecrow's horse the sod was removed in horse-track shaped sections consecutively from the point of advance from the village round the place of combat and returning to the village. The horse-track marks were made about two feet in diameter. All these marks commemorating the entire action, which took place about the year 1853 are still plainly evident, being renewed whenever they tend to become obliterated by weathering and by advancing vegetation.

THE LEGEND OF STANDING ROCK

This story of Standing Rock is a legend of the Arikara who once had their villages along the Missouri River between the Grand River and the Cannonball River. Afterwards, being harrassed by hostile incursions of the Dakotas they abandoned this country to their enemies and moved farther up the Missouri River, joining themselves in alliance with the Mandans.

One time there was a young girl in this tribe who was beautiful and amiable but not given to heedless, chattering, idle amusement. She was thoughtful and earnest and conversant with the ways of all the living creatures, the birds and the small mammals, and the trees and shrubs and flowers of the woodlands and of the prairies. She was in the habit of going to walk by herself to visit and commune with all these living creatures. She understood them better than most other people did, and they all were her friends.

When she became of marriageable age she had many suitors, for she was beautiful and lovely in disposition. But to the young men who wooed her she answered, "I do not find it in my heart to marry any one. I am at home with the bird people, the four-footed people of the woods and prairies, with the people of the flower nations and the trees. I love to work in the cornfields in summer, and the sacred squash blossoms are my dear companions."

Finally her grandmother reasoned with her and told her that it was her duty to marry and to rear children to maintain the strength of the tribe. Because of filial duty she finally said, when her grandmother continued to urge her to marry a certain young man of estimable worth who desired her for his wife, "Well grandmother, I will obey you, but I tell you that good will not come of it. I am not as others are, and Mother Nature did not intend me for marriage."

So she was married and went to the house already prepared for her by her husband. But three days later she came back to her mother's, house, appearing sad and downcast. She sat down without speaking. Finally her grandmother said, "What is it, my child? Is he not kind to you?" The girl answered, "Oh, no, he is not unkind. He treated me well." And with that she sped away into the forest. Her grandmother followed her after a little while, thinking that out among her beloved trees and plants she might open her heart and tell her what was the trouble. And this she did, explaining all the trouble to her grandmother. And she concluded her talk with her grandmother with these words, saying: "And so you see, grandmother, it is as I said when you urged me to marry. I was not intended for marriage. And now my heart is so sad. I should not have married. My spirit is not suited to the bounds of ordinary human living, and my husband is not to be blamed. He is honorable and kind. But I must go away and be with the children of nature." So her grandmother left her there where she was sitting by a clump of choke-cherries, having her sewing kit with her and her little dog by her side.

She did not return home that night, so the next morning young men were sent to search for her. At last she was found sitting upon a hill out upon the prairie, and she was turned to stone from her feet to her waist. The young men hastened back to the village and reported to the officers who had sent them out.

Then the people were summoned by the herald and they all went out to the place where the young woman was. Now they found she had become stone as far up as her breasts.

Then the priests opened the sacred bundle and took the sacred pipe which they filled and lighted and presented it to her lips so that thus she and they in turn smoking from the same pipe might be put in communion and accord with the spirit. But she refused the pipe, and said, "Though I refuse the pipe it is not from disloyalty or because of unwillingness to be at one with my people; but I am different by nature. And you shall know my good will towards my people and my love and remembrance of them always, for whoever in summer time places by this stone a wild flower or a twig of a living tree in winter time or any such token of living, wonderful Nature at any time, shall be glad in his heart, and shall have his desire to be in communion with the heart of Nature." And as she said these words she turned completely into stone, and her little dog, sitting at her feet and leaning close against her was also turned into stone with her. And this stone is still to be seen, and is revered by the people. It is from this stone that the country around Fort Yates, North Dakota, is called Standing Rock.

THE HOLY HILL PAHUK

Each of the nations and tribes of Indians had certain places within its own domain which they regarded as sacred, and to which they accordingly paid becoming reverence. These places were sometimes watersprings, sometimes peculiar hills, sometimes caves, sometimes rocky precipices, sometimes dark, wooded bluffs. Within the ancient domain of the Pawnee nation in Nebraska and northwest Kansas there is a cycle of five such sacred places. The chief one of these five mystic places is called Pahuk by the Pawnee. From its nature it is unique, being distinctly different from any other hill in all the Pawnee country. Pahuk stands in a bend of the Platte River where the stream flows from the west in a sweep abruptly turning toward the southeast. The head of the hill juts out into the course of the river like a promontory or headland, which is the literal meaning of the Pawnee word "pahuk." The north face of the bluff from the water's edge to the summit is heavily wooded. Among the timber are many cedar trees, so that in winter, when the deciduous trees are bare, the bluff is dark with the mass of evergreen cedar. The cedar is a sacred tree, so its presence adds mystery to the place. The Pawnee sometimes also speak of this hill as Nahura Waruksti, which means Sacred or Mysterious Animals. This allusion to the Sacred or Mysterious Animals has reference to the myth which pertains to this place.

All the other tribes throughout the Great Plains region also knew of the veneration in which this hill is held by the Pawnee, so they, too, pay it great respect, and many individuals of the other tribes have personally made pilgrimages to this holy place. The people of the Dakota nation call it Paha Wakan, "the Holy Hill."

The Pawnee speak of the animal world collectively as Nahurak. It was believed that the interrelations of all living beings, plants, animals and human beings, are essentially harmonious, and that all species take a wholesome interest in each other's welfare. It was believed also that under certain conditions ability was given to different orders of living creatures to communicate with men for man's good.

The before-mentioned five sacred places of the Pawnee country were Nahurak lodges. Within these mystic secret places the animals, Nahurak, held council. According to one version the names of the five Nahurak lodges are Pahuk, Nakiskat, Tsuraspako, Kitsawitsak, and Pahua. Pahuk is a bluff on the south side of the Platte River, a few miles west of the city of Fremont, Nebraska; Nakiskat, (Black trees) is an island in the Platte River near Central City, Nebraska, dark with cedar trees; Tsuraspako (Girl Hill) is a hill on the south side of the Platte River opposite Grand Island, Nebraska. It is called Girl Hill because it was customary when a buffalo surround was made in its vicinity for the young girls to stay upon this hill during the surround. The hill is said to be in the form of an earth-lodge, even to the extended vestibule. Kitsawitsak, which white people call Wakonda Springs, is not far from the Solomon River near Beloit, Kansas. The name Kitsawitsak means "Water on the bank." Pahua is said to be a spring near the Republican River in Nebraska. Of these five places Pahuk was chief, and the Nahurak councils of the other lodges acknowledged the superior authority of the council at Pahuk.

There are many stories of the wonderful powers resident in these sacred places. One of these tells of the restoration to life of a boy who had been killed. The story is that a certain man of the Skidi tribe of the Pawnee nation desired to gain the favour of Tirawa (Pawnee name of God). He thought that if he sacrificed something which he valued most highly that Tirawa might grant him some wonderful gift. There were so many things in the world which he did not understand, and which he wished very much to know. He hoped that Tirawa might grant him revelations, that he might know and understand many things which were hidden from the people. He strongly desired knowledge, and he thought that if he sacrificed his young son, who was dear to him, and the pride of his heart, that Tirawa might take pity on him and grant him his desire. He felt very sad to think of killing his son, and he meditated a long time upon the matter. Finally he was convinced in his own mind that Tirawa would be pleased with his sacrifice, and that then the good gifts he desired would be given to him, and that many things now dark to his understanding would be made clear, and that he should have ability given him to do many things which were now beyond his power.

One day this man took his boy with him and walked out from the village as though on some errand. They walked to the Platte River. After they had gone a long distance from the village, as they were walking by the riverside, no other persons being near, the man drew out his knife and stabbed the boy so that he was quickly dead. The man then dropped the body of the dead boy over the bank. After a time he returned to the village, and went into his own lodge and sat down. After a while he asked his wife "Where is the boy?" She said "Why, he went out with you." The man said "I was out of the village, but the boy was not with me."

He went out and inquired of his neighbors, and then all through the village, but of course the boy could not be found. Then for some days a general search was made for the boy, but no trace of him was found. After this the family mourned for the lost boy. It was now time for the summer buffalo hunt, so in a few days the people set out for the buffalo grounds, and the father and mother of the boy also went.

After the boy's body was dropped into the river it was carried away down-stream by the current, sometimes being rolled along in shallow water at the edge of sandbars and again it would be turned over and over in the whirlpool of some deep hole in the channel, for the Platte River is a peculiar stream, having a swift current but a wide course with deep holes and many sandbars.

After a time the body floated down nearly to Pahuk. Two buzzards were sitting on the edge of a bluff, gazing over the water. So, sitting there, one of the buzzards stretched out his neck and looked up the river. He thought he saw something in the water floating down-stream. He stretched his neck again and looked, and turned to the other buzzard and said "I see a body." Then they both looked towards the object in the water, stretching out their necks and gazing intently. They saw that the object was the body of the boy. The first one said "What shall we do about this?" The second one said "Let us carry the body down to Pahuk, to the hill where Nahurak Waruksti is." So they both flew down to the floating body and got under it and lifted it upon their backs and carried it to the top of the bluff called Pahuk, over the secret cave of the Nahurak Waruksti, and there they placed it upon the ground. Then the two buzzards stood quietly gazing upon the body of the boy where they had laid it down upon the ground.

This cave far under the hill was the council lodge of the animals. There sat the councilmen of all kinds of animals and birds, great and small, which were native to that country. There were the buffalo, the beaver, elk, deer, antelope, otter, muskrat, wolf, bear, fox, wildcat, badger, bean mice, and many other kinds of animals. And there were the swan, the loon, goose, duck, wild turkey, prairie chicken, quail, heron, bittern, crane, plover, kildeer, meadowlark, blackbird, owls, hawks, swallows, crow, chickadee, woodpeckers, grackle, purple martin, and many other kinds of birds. There were also snakes, turtles, toads and frogs. These were the Nahurak people, the Nahurak Waruksti, the Sacred Animals. And the kingfisher was a messenger and errand man for the Nahurak council.

Now it happened when the buzzards brought the body of the young man and laid it down on the top of Pahuk, the kingfisher, who was flying about over the river on business for the Nahurak, was flying by. He stopped and looked at the body. He already knew all that had happened, and he was moved with compassion for the boy. So he flew down at once to the water at the foot of Pahuk and dived in at the entrance of the Nahurak lodge. He spoke to the assembly of the Nahurak and told them all that had happened and said in conclusion, "And the poor boy is up there on the hill. I hope you will have pity on him and will do what you can for him. I wish you would bring him to life again." When the kingfisher, the messenger, had finished speaking the Nahurak held serious council on the matter to decide what they should do. But after they had meditated long on the question, and each had spoken, they still could not decide the matter. The kingfisher urged the matter, asking for a favourable decision, saying, "Come, do take pity on him and restore him to life." But they could not come to a decision. At last the chief of the council said, "No, messenger, we are unable to decide now. You must go to the other Nahurak lodges and find out what they have to say about it." The kingfisher said "I go," and flew swiftly out from the lodge and up the river to Nakiskat, the Nahurak lodge near Lone Tree. There he brought the matter before the council and pleaded for the boy as he had done at Pahuk, and told them that he was sent from Pahuk to ask the council at Nakiskat for their decision. So the Nahurak here at Nakiskat talked over the matter, but at last they said to the kingfisher "We are unable to decide. We leave it to the council at Pahuk."

Then the kingfisher flew to the lodge at Tsuraspako, then to Kitsawitsak, and at last to Pahua, and at each place the Nahurak council considered the matter carefully and talked about it, but at each place the same answer was given. They all said "It is too much for us. We cannot decide what should be done. It is for the council at Pahuk to decide."

After the messenger had visited all these lodges and had laid the matter before all of them, receiving from each the same answer, he flew as swiftly as he could back to the lodge at Pahuk and reported what the other lodges had said. They all recognized the council at Pahuk as the head council, and deferred the matter to them for decision. But it had already been once considered by this council, so the matter was now brought before the supreme council of Pahuk. This was a council of four chiefs of the Pahuk council who sat as judges to give final consideration and decision. These judges now reconsidered the matter, and finally, when they had talked it over, they said to the kingfisher, "Now, messenger, we will not decide this question, but will leave it to you. You shall make the decision."

The kingfisher very quickly gave his decision. He said "It is my desire that this poor boy be restored to life. I hope you will all have pity on him and do what you can for him."

Then all the Nahurak arose and went out from the council lodge and went up to the top of Pahuk where the body of the boy lay. They formed in order and stood around the boy and prayed to the Higher Powers, and at last the boy drew breath, then after a time he breathed again, then his breath began to be regular. Finally he opened his eyes and sat up and looked around in a confused manner. When he saw all the animals standing around him he was puzzled and bewildered. He said to himself, "Why, my father killed me by the riverside, but here I am in the midst of this multitude of animals. What does it mean?"

Then the head chief of the Nahurak council spoke to him kindly and reassured him. He was asked to rise and go with the animals into the council lodge. When all had gone in and were seated the four judges conferred together, then the chief of the four stood up and said, "My people, we have restored this boy to life, but he is poor and forlorn and needy. Let us do something for him. Let us teach him all we know, and impart to him our mysterious powers." The Nahurak were all pleased at this proposal and manifested their approval.

Then the Nahurak showed hospitality and kind attention to the poor boy as their guest. He was shown a place to bathe and rest. When he had rested, food was brought to him. So he was entertained and treated kindly for the full season, and he was instructed by all the animals in turn and they taught him their secret arts of healing and imparted to him all their wonderful powers. So he remained with them at Pahuk till autumn.

Autumn is a beautiful season at Pahuk, and in all the region of the Platte, the Loup, the Republican, and the Solomon rivers in Nebraska and Kansas embraced by the cycle of the five Nahurak lodges. At that season in that country the sun casts a mellow golden light from the sky, while the land is emblazed with the brilliance of the sunflowers and goldenrod. And then the air is quiet and restful.

So one day at this season the Nahurak said to the boy, "It is now the time when the swallows, the blackbirds, the meadowlarks, and other kinds of birds will be gathering into flocks to fly away to the south-land for the winter. The beavers are cutting trees and saplings to store the branches under water for their winter food supply of bark; they are also gathering into their houses certain kinds of roots for food. The muskrats are repairing their houses and are storing in them the tubers of the water-lilies and of the arrow-leaf and of other kinds of plants for their winter supply. In the edge of the timber, where the ground beans grow, the bean mice are making their store-houses and filling them with ground beans and artichokes. And your people have returned from the buffalo hunt with a good supply of dried meat and hides. They are now busy at home gathering and storing their crops of corn, of beans, and of squashes and pumpkins. We have this past summer instructed you in our arts of healing and other learning, and have imparted to you our mysterious powers, and have taught you about our ways of living. You are now competent to use for the good of your people the remedies and perform the mysteries which were given to us by Tirawa, and which we have now given to you. So you may now return to the village of your people. Go to the chiefs of the village and tell them what the Nahurak have done for you, and say to them that the people are to bring together gifts of dried buffalo meat and dried corn and dried choke-cherries, and other kinds of food; of robes and leggings and moccasins embroidered with porcupine quills; and of tobacco for incense. All these things the people are to send by you as gifts to the Nahurak at Pahuk in recognition of the favour which the Nahurak showed to you."

So the boy parted from his animal friends at Pahuk, and promised to return and visit them, and to bring them presents to show his thankfulness and the thankfulness of his people for what the animals had done for him. He traveled on up the Platte River and reached the village of his people in the night. He went to his father's house. He found his father and mother asleep and the fire had burned low. There was only a little light from the coals. He went to his mother's bed and touched her shoulder and spoke to her to waken her. He said "It is I. I have come back." When his mother saw him and heard his voice she was surprised, but she was glad-hearted to see her boy again. So she wakened the boy's father and told him the boy had come back. When the father saw the boy he thought it must be his ghost, and he was afraid. But the boy did not mention anything that had happened nor say where he had been. He said only "I have come back again."

The next day some of the people saw him, and they were surprised. They told their neighbors, and soon it was rumored all over the village that the boy had returned. They came where he was and stood around and looked at him and asked him questions, but he told them nothing. But he went to the chiefs of the village and made his report to them. Afterwards he gave account to the people, saying, "I have been away all summer with friends, with people who have been very good to me. Now I should like to take them a present of dried meat and other good things, so that we can have a feast. I beg you to help me, my friends." So they brought together a quantity of the articles required, and they chose some young men to go with him to help carry the gifts to the people who had befriended him.

So the boy and his companions went on the way towards the Nahurak lodge at Pahuk. When they came near to the place the boy dismissed the young men who had accompanied him, and they went back to the village. Now the boy went on alone and met the kingfisher, the messenger of the Nahurak, and sent word by him that he had come to visit the Nahurak, and had brought presents from his people. So the boy was invited into the lodge and all the Nahurak made sounds of gladness at seeing him again. The boy brought in the presents which had been sent by his people and they had a feast. After the feast they held a doctors' ceremony. They reviewed all the things that the Nahurak had taught him during the summer that he had spent with them. Then the boy was made a doctor, and he was now able to do many wonderful things.

After this the time came for the young man to return again to the village of his people. The animals were thankful and gave praise to Tirawa for the gifts which the young man had brought to them. And the young man was thankful to the animals and he praised Tirawa for what the animals had done for him. Then he returned to the village of his people. He never told the people what his father had done to him.

The young man lived a long and useful life among his people and attained much honour. He did many wonderful things for his people and healed them of their diseases and injuries. In time he gathered about him a group of other young men, who, like himself, were of serious and thoughtful mind, and who had desire toward the welfare of the people. These young men became his disciples, and to them he taught the mysteries which had been imparted to him by the animals of the lodge at Pahuk. These wise men in turn taught other worthy inquirers, and these again others; and so these mysteries and learning and the healing arts have come down from that long-ago time to the present among the Pawnee people.

THE LODGE OF THE BLACK-TAIL DEER WHICH TALKED WITH ITS CAPTOR

North Dakota has a number of places to which attach interesting legends and myths. One such place is a butte not far from Schmitt on the south side of the Missouri River on the road between Mandan and Cannon Ball. It is west of Eagle-beak Butte.

The story of this butte is a Mandan myth. A long time ago the Mandans lived in a village which was on a level place just north of the Bad Water Creek, which white people call Little Heart River. At the west of this place there is a range of high hills. The Mandans lived at the Bad Water Village in the time long before white men had come across the great water, so there were no horses in the country. The people had no animals except dogs to help them carry their burdens. And of course they had never heard of the thunder-irons (guns) which strike and kill the deer and other game at long distance. So it was hard work to obtain their supplies of meat and to carry the same home to their houses.

A man who lived in the Bad Water village had dug a deer pit in a place among the hills west of the village and cunningly covered it over to appear not different from the ground about it. By this means he hoped to capture a deer whose flesh would be food for his family, and whose skin would be useful for making clothing; whose sinew would be used for thread, some of its bones to be used for making awls and needles, others for other useful implements and tools. Its horns would be used to make garden rakes for working the ground of his family's garden.

One morning in autumn there had been a snowfall during the preceding night, the first snowfall of the season. The man went out early in the morning into the hills to look at his trap to see if it might have caught something during the night. As he approached the place he saw that the cover was broken through, and when he came near and looked in he was rejoiced to see that he had captured a fine large black-tail deer.

Now when he came to the edge of the pit and looked down at his prize the deer looked up at him and spoke to him, saying, "O, man, do not kill me, but let me go free from the pit. If you release me you will do well." The man was surprised to hear the deer speak to him like a man, and he was disappointed to think of losing his prize. But he thought to himself, "This is something mysterious, I must give heed; I must not defy the Mysterious Power, but listen to the message; for it must be that some Mysterious Power wishes to impart something to me through this animal as its messenger." So as he thus hesitated in doubt the deer again made its plea and requested to be set free. But the man spoke of his duty to his family, who looked to him for food and for clothing. Again the deer spoke and said, "Indeed you do well to think of your family, and your endeavor to provide for them as well as you can is prompted both by your love and duty. But I say to you that you would do well if you allow me to go. If you do so, I promise you that you will have success in hunting; you shall find game abundant for the needs of yourself and family. And when war comes upon your people you shall be victorious over the enemy. So shall you be remembered among your people for bravery."

 The man gave heed to what the deer said to him, and he dared not disobey the message which had come to him in this mysterious way. So now he began to dig down the side of the pit so that the deer could come out. When he had finished he said to the deer, "Now you may go." Then the deer came up the incline from the pit and ran down across the Bad Water Creek away toward the Eagle Beak Hill. As he ran the new fallen snow flew behind him from his hoofs in a white cloud, and he sang a song:

"I was glad when I saw the first snow,But I almost lost the sight of day."

The man watched the deer as it ran and observed that when it approached a conical butte west of Eagle-beak Butte that the butte opened with a loud roaring sound and the deer entered and he saw it no more, and then the butte closed again as before.

The man went home pondering these things in his mind. As time passed events came true as they had been promised to him in the message spoken to him by the deer. He became renowned among his people for his skill and success in the chase, for his generosity to the old people and to the sick and poor, and he attained many honors for his deeds of valour in warfare against the enemies of his people.

Ever since that time the Mandans have called the butte into which the deer disappeared after its release from the pit, The Lodge of the Black-tail Deer.

THE WONDERFUL BASKET

A Mandan Story

Indians of all tribes held the thought of the brotherhood of all living nature, of the trees and flowers and grasses, of the fishes in the waters, of the living things which creep or walk or run on the land and of the birds which fly above the earth, and of human beings. And they believed that human beings often gained wisdom and useful information through dreams and visions in which the guardian spirits of any of these other living creatures talked to them, revealing to chosen, attentive and worthy persons, secrets of nature which were hidden from the careless and unworthy.

Among most tribes the cedar tree is considered to possess a property of mystery and sacredness. For this reason twigs of cedar were often burned as incense in a sacred fire for the purpose of driving away evil influences. And if a person reclined under the shelter of cedar trees the healing power and strength of their spirit would come to him and his own spirit would thus gain composure and strength to meet life's troubles.

Once in the old times a woman was resting under a cedar tree. She was weary from her work, and as the gentle wind sighed among the thick green branches above her she dropped to sleep. While she slept the cedar tree spoke to her in a soft murmuring voice, and the woman gave heed to the words of the cedar tree.

And this is what the cedar tree said to the woman: "Sister, if you will dig down into the earth you will find there my slender, strong, pliant roots. Take up some of these and weave them into a basket. You shall find thereafter that some good shall come of it. It shall bring good to you and to all women."

So the woman did as she was told by the cedar tree. She took up the slender roots and wove of them a basket. The basket was light but strong, and so pliant that it could be rolled into a small bundle when empty, though it was large enough to hold many things when it was opened out.

One day the woman took the basket with her and walked far out upon the prairie where tipsin grew in abundance. She dug a quantity of the sweet and wholesome roots to take home for food for herself and her family. The tipsin roots grow so deep in the tough prairie sod that it is hard work to dig them, so when she had filled her basket she was very tired. She sat down to rest and sighed for very weariness, and the tears came to her eyes. She said, "Alas! now I must carry home this heavy load although I am already weary and faint."

Then the basket whispered to her "Do not cry. Wipe away your tears; bathe your hot cheeks with water at the brook; be glad, for I am your friend."

Then the woman wiped away her tears and went and bathed her cheeks and brushed her hair. When she returned the basket seemed to smile. It said to her "You were troubled for nothing. You forget what the cedar tree said to you in your dreams. You were told that good would come to you if you made a basket as you were instructed. Now you need not carry your load; but sing and be glad and walk on to the village. I shall come with you, carrying your load."

So the woman went on her way home, singing from happiness, while the basket kept by her side carrying the load of tipsin roots.

As she came near the village the women knew by her happy singing voice that some good thing had happened to her. Then as they looked up they saw her coming, and with her was coming the wonderful basket carrying the load.

Then all her neighbors begged her to teach them how to make a wonderful basket. So she taught them as she had been taught by the holy cedar tree how to make a wonderful basket out of its tiny roots.

And so, from that time, whenever a woman went out to gather June berries or wild cherries, or raspberries, or wild plums or pembinas or tipsin, or wild rice; or to their cultivated fields to gather corn or beans, she was not obliged to carry the load home. When she was ready she started towards the village singing, and the basket came with her cheerfully carrying the burden.

One day, long after this, a woman had found the winter store-house of the hintunka people, which they make under-ground, and into which they garner their store of food for the winter time. The hard-working hintunka people put away in their store-houses quantities of wild ground beans, various kinds of seeds and roots and tubers to provide themselves food for the cold time when the ground is frozen and the earth is covered with snow.

It happened that the woman who found this store-house of the hintunka people was one who was not considerate of the rights of other people. She thought only that here was a quantity of food which was desirable and easy to obtain. So she filled her basket with the wild ground beans which are so delicious when cooked with bits of meat. She cared not that it had cost the hintunka people many weary hours of hard work to dig these beans and bring them together in this place, nor did she care that without them the hintunka people, their old people and their little ones, all would be left destitute of food and must perish from famine.

While she was filling her basket a poor little hintunka woman cried pitifully and said, "This is our food. We have worked hard for it. You ought not to rob us of it. Without it we shall die miserably of hunger." But the woman took the beans and heeded not the pitiful crying of the hintunka woman. She had filled her basket, and was making ready to go home but there was no song in her heart.

Then, while the filled basket sat there waiting a coyote standing near by, laughed. At this the basket was vexed, and said, "You are rude. Why do you laugh at me?" But the coyote only laughed all the more. This annoyed the basket greatly, and made it feel very uneasy and distressed, for it knew something must be wrong. And it said to the coyote, "Do tell me why you laugh. What is it which is strange?"

Then the coyote replied, "I laugh because you are so foolish. For a long time you have been carrying burdens to the village while the women go their way singing."

But the basket said, "I am not foolish, I have the good spirit of the cedar tree. I am willing to carry burdens to help the women. I am glad when I hear their joyful singing." The coyote said, "But what do you get for it, friend? You work like a slave. You receive nothing for it. No one offers you a mouthful of food. When you rest for a time from your labor you are not covered with a robe made beautiful with quill-work. When you have carried burdens for a woman she merely hangs you upon a peg on the wall till the next time she wishes you to carry something for her."

As the basket considered the things which the coyote said it began to be discontented. It felt that it had been treated unfairly; that it had no pay nor thanks for all it had done, and so the basket was sulky, and refused to carry the load to the village, and the woman at last had to take up the burden and carry it upon her back; and she felt aggrieved and bitter because the basket would not carry it for her. She did not consider that all the service she had ever had from the basket was from kindness and good will and not from obligation.

And ever since that time the women have had to carry burdens upon their backs, for the baskets no longer carried burdens for them.

CAUSE OF THE BREAKING UP OF THE ICE IN THE MISSOURI RIVER IN SPRINGTIME

A Myth of the Dakota Nation

It is said that in the long ago there was a mysterious being within the stream of the Missouri River. It was seldom seen by human beings, and was most dreadful to see. It is said that sometimes it was seen within the water in the middle of the stream, causing a redness shining like the redness of fire as it passed up the stream against the current with a terrific roaring sound.

And they say that if this dreadful being was seen by anyone in the daytime anyone who thus saw it soon after became crazy and continued restless and writhing as though in pain until he was relieved by death. And it is said that one time not a very great many years ago this frightful being was seen by a man, and he told how it appeared. He said that it was of strange form and covered all over with hair like a buffalo, but red in color; that it had only one eye in the middle of its forehead, and above that a single horn. Its backbone stood out notched and jagged like an enormous saw. As soon as the man beheld the awful sight everything became dark to him, he said. He was just able to reach home, but he lost his reason and soon after that he died.

It is said this mysterious "Miniwashitu" (water monster) still lives in the Missouri River, and that in springtime, as it moves up-stream against the current it breaks up the ice of the river. This water monster was held in awe and dread by the people.

THE WATER-SPRING OF THE HOLY MAN

A Myth of the Dakota Nation

Long ago there was a village of people of the Dakota Nation, which was situated on the east side of the great river which they call the Muddy-Water River, but which white people call the Missouri River. The white people named it so from the Missouri nation of Indians on the lower course of this great river.

This village we have just mentioned was on the east side of the river nearly opposite to the mouth of the Cannonball River. The people were happy in this village, for it was a pleasant place. There was plenty of wood for their fires, and there was an abundance of buffalo berries, wild plums, choke-cherries, June berries, wild grapes, wild raspberries and other fruit growing in the woods. Upon the high prairie there was much tipsin, whose roots are so good when cooked with meat or with dried green corn. Moreover, in the timber were many boxelder trees, whose sap was made into sugar in early spring time. Not far away were some lakes where there were many wild ducks and geese and other water fowl. The flesh of these fowl, and also their eggs were good food. Upon the prairie were herds of buffalo and antelope and elk, and in the timber along the river were many deer.

And below the hills, on the level ground of the river valley there was fertile soil where they planted their fields of corn and beans and squashes. They also cultivated the great sunflowers whose seeds are so good for food.

And the people loved this place, for besides all the good things to eat, and other comforts which it gave them, it was also pleasant to look upon. There was the mysterious river coming down from the distant mountains away in the west and flowing on towards the lands of other nations of people in the south, and whose channel could be seen winding its gleaming way among the dark trees on its shores. Upon the prairie hills in early spring the courageous little pasque flowers appeared like a gray-blue cloud let down upon the hill-tops where they nodded their cheery greetings to the people who passed them. A little later in the little vales were masses of deep blue violets. Still later the prairie was bright with the colour and the air was sweet with the breath of the wild rose of the prairie. The cheery meadowlark, which the people call the bird of promise, flitted here and there and called his greetings and promised good things to his friends, the Dakota people.

And through the procession of the seasons there were spread out before their eyes on all sides scenes of beauty, changing with the change of seasons and changing every day, indeed the beauties of colour and light and shade were changing at every stage of the day from the rosy dawn till the blue shades of evening came.

Yes, it was a delightful land and the people rejoiced in it. But a strange thing happened which caused the people to move away to a far distant place. And this is the way it happened:

There was living in this village an old man, a wise man, a man who was held in great respect by the people, for he was a holy man, to whom the Unseen Powers granted knowledge not given to all the people. And these revelations came to the holy man in visions.

This holy man was now too old and feeble to till the soil and raise crops of food plants, or to go on the chase for game, or to gather any of the wild food plants. But because they held him in honor the young men were glad to provide for him, and the women cooked for him of the best they had.

But one time he had a vision which made him very sad, so that he could only cry and weep and could not speak of his vision for sadness of heart.

And the people besought him to tell them his vision, for, they said, "if it is a vision of evil to come, we may as well know the worst. We ought to be prepared for it." For a long time the old man could not bring himself to tell them the evil foreboding which had come to him. But at last, when they continued strongly urging him to tell them what it was, he said: "Well, my children, I will tell you the vision, for it may be that I shall not live long. This vision has come to me from the Mysterious and Awful Powers, and it is full of evil portent for our people." But now he was again so overcome by sadness that he was unable to tell it.

Again, after some days the people begged him to tell the vision, and they pressed him so urgently that finally he said: "This is what I saw in my vision, which has come to me repeatedly. I saw a great incursion of human beings of strange appearance. They are coming from the direction of the rising sun and are moving toward this land in multitudes so great that they cannot be counted. They move everywhere over the face of the land like the restless fluctuations of heated air which are sometimes seen incessantly wavering over the heated prairie on a summer day. They are moving on resistlessly toward us and nothing can stop them, and they will take our land from us. They are a terrible people and of a monstrous appearance. The skin of this people is not of a wholesome color like the skin of our people who are born of our holy mother earth. Their skin is hideous and ghastly, and the men have hairy faces like the face of a wolf. They are not kind like our people; they are savages, cruel and unfeeling. They have no reverence for our holy places, nor for our holy mother earth. And they kill and destroy all things and make the land desolate. They have no ear for the voices of the trees and the flowers, and no pity for the birds and the beasts of the field. And they deface and spoil the beauty of the land and befoul the water courses.

"And they have many dreadful customs. When a person dies the body is not honorably laid upon a funeral scaffold on the prairie or in the branches of a tree in the forest as we do, but they dig a hole in the ground and put the body down into the hole and then fill the hole up again, throwing the dirt down upon the body. And they have strange and powerful weapons, so that when they come our people will not be able to withstand them. It is this dreadful vision which has overcome me with sadness."

Then the people were amazed and angry. They tried to have him change his vision, but he could not. Again the same vision came to him. The leading men now counseled and gave the order that the people should give him no more food for some days. They said, "Perhaps he will have a different vision." So he was left alone in his tent for four days. And on the fourth day when they came to his tent they found him dead. They had not intended to cause his death, but they hoped that if they let him become very hungry he would change his vision.

Now when they found him dead they were shocked and astonished and very angry. They said, "Now the evil which he foretold will come, for he died without changing his vision." And they said "We will not bury him honorably upon a scaffold according to our custom, but we will bury him in a hole in the ground, as he said his 'wandering people' bury their dead." So they dug a hole and into this they put the body of the old man and put the earth back again upon the body.

At evening some women were gazing out across the river in the twilight, and they saw a man come up out of the river and advance toward the village. When he came nearer they saw it was the holy man who had died and whose body had been buried in a hole in the ground. When he died he had changed from this life to the life of those who dwell in "The Land of Evening Mirage." From the place where they buried him he had gone out under the ground and had come up out of the water of the river. Now when he came up out from the water he was changed back again to the life on earth. From this it was evident to all the people that he was indeed a very holy man, and that his vision was true and must come to pass. They gave him a good dwelling and provided for all his needs, and the women cooked for him the best food they had, and every one did homage to him and paid him reverence.

After a time he knew that the end of his life was approaching, and as he was about to die he called the leading men about him and said, "The vision which I had will truly come to pass in future time. Now I am about to die. When I am dead let me be buried in the ground again at the place where I was buried before. You will see that some good thing will come of it for our people at this place. And it shall be good for all people at this place forever." When he said something good would come they thought he meant that the people should be saved from the cruel and savage, strange, pale-skinned people of his vision, but that was not what he meant.

When the holy man was dead they would have preferred to give him honorable scaffold burial as was customary, but they did as he had directed and buried him in the ground where he had been buried before. But this time, they dug out a roomy place, and made walls and a roof with timbers, and in this place they put the body of the holy man after dressing him in the best of garments decorated with porcupine quill embroidery, and wrapped in a fine buffalo robe painted with beautiful designs. And they placed with him his pipe and tobacco and food and valuable presents of all kinds. Then they covered it all over with earth again and set the sod as it was before.

At evening they watched the place in the river where he had reappeared the other time after his burial. They thought he might return again out of the water of the river, but he did not come. And they listened above the little house they had made for him under the ground, but they heard not the slightest sound of breathing or any movement. Then they made a sacred fire by the grave from twigs of the cedar tree, for this tree is holy and sacred to the Good Powers and the breath of its fire will bring persons of good intention into communion with those Unseen Powers. But the holy man did not appear by the sacred fire and he was never seen again by any of the people.

Now the people became so burdened with sadness that they could not endure to remain at this place, so they moved far away, where they found another good country. In this new place they stayed until all the people who were grown at the time they left the village of the holy man's grave, had become old and had died. And none had ever been back there. Then, when all those who were but boys and girls when they left the former village had now become old men and women, their tribe began to suffer harrassment from an enemy people of another tribe. Their enemies were too strong for them, so they had to think of moving to another place. And so it came into their minds to return to the place by the Muddy-Water River, where they had lived at the time when those of their people who were now old had been merry, happy children.

So they came back, and before they had reached the place the old men said, "Let us go on ahead and see the grave of the holy man." And when the old men came to the place where the holy man had been buried they found that a spring of good water issued from the place where the holy man's grave had been. And that is why we call this spring "The Holy Man's Waterspring."

And it is said that now a bright star is often seen shining over this spring for a while and that it then goes down and disappears into the water of the spring. And it is said that sometimes when the moon is full and bright the holy man may be seen walking near the spring. When one approaches to speak to him he disappears into the spring. Not all persons can see these things, but only those whose hearts are kind and gentle, and whose minds are in accord with Nature, and who have reverence for holy things and for the beauties and mysteries in Nature.

THE SACRED SYMBOL OF THE CIRCLE

To the Dakotas the form of the circle is a sacred symbol because Great Spirit caused everything in nature except stone to be round. Stone is the implement of destruction. The sun, the earth and the moon are round like a shield, and the sky is round like a bowl inverted over the earth. All breathing creatures are round like a human body. All things growing out of the ground are round, as the trunk of a tree or the stem of an herb. The edge of the world is a circle, hence the circle is a symbol of the world and of the winds which travel to us from all points on the edge of the world. The sun and the moon which mark the day and the night travel in a circle above the sky; for this reason the circle is a symbol of these divisions of time, and of the year, and so is the symbol for all time.

Raindrops are round, and so are the drops of dew hanging like strings of beads upon the grass blades. Pellets of hail and of sleet are round. Every snowflake has a centre from which lines radiate as from the centre of a circle. The rainbow, which beautifies the sky after showers, is round.

Because Great Spirit has caused almost all things to be round it is for us a sacred symbol; it reminds us of the work of Great Spirit in the universe. And for this reason Dakotas make their tipis round; and in laying a camp the tipis are set in a circular line; and in all ceremonies they sit in a circle.

The circle is a symbol of the tipi and of shelter and comfort. In decorative figures the undivided circle is a symbol of the world and of time. If the circle be filled with red it is a symbol of the sun; if filled with blue it is a symbol of the sky. If the circle be divided into four parts it is a symbol of the four winds.

The mouthpiece of a pipe should always be passed about the circle and offered to the four directions before it is formally smoked.

THE SACRED NUMBER FOUR

It appears that Great Spirit caused everything in the world to be in fours; for this reason mankind's activities of all kinds should be governed by the number four out of respect to this sacred number and in agreement with it.

We see that there are four directions: the north, the east, the south, and the west; four divisions of time: the day, the night, the moon, and the year; there are four seasons: the spring, the summer, the autumn, and the winter; there are four parts to everything that grows from the ground: the roots, the stems, the leaves, and the fruits; four kinds of things that breathe: those that crawl, those that fly, those that walk on four legs, and those that walk on two legs; four things above the world: the sun, the moon, the sky, and the stars; four kinds of gods: the great, the associates of the great, the gods below them, and the spirit kind; four periods of human life: infancy, youth, adulthood, and old age; mankind has four fingers on each hand, four toes on each foot, and the thumbs and big toes of each taken together make four.

All these tokens of the works of Great Spirit should cause mankind to order his ceremonies and all activities so far as possible by this sacred number.

THE PRISTINE PRAIRIE

To obtain even an approximate appreciation of the conditions of life as they presented themselves to the people of the nations which formerly occupied the region drained by the Missouri River and its tributaries we must bring ourselves to see it as it was in its natural condition, void of all the countless changes and accessories which we have erected here by our European culture and custom.

Imagine, then, a country of open prairie stretching away and away beyond the range of vision over hill, valley, and plain, the skyline unbroken by trees, except a fringe along the course of the streams. The aspect of this landscape in summer was that of a boundless sea of shining green, billowing under the prevailing south wind, darkened here and there by the swiftly marching shadows of clouds sailing high and white in the brilliant blue sky. Toward the end of summer the sun appears to have shed some of its lustre upon the plain below, for it now shines with a paler light, while the ever restless, rustling, whispering sea of grass waves in rolling billows of golden green, seeming to be forever flowing on before the south wind into the mysterious North, changing again into yellow and warm brown as autumn comes on.

Then it may happen some day that the whole aspect is suddenly changed. Fire has escaped in the sea of dry grass. To the windward the horizon is one long line of smoke, which, as it comes nearer, rolls up in black masses shot through with darting tongues of angry red flames leaping a hundred feet skyward, while the sound of the conflagration is like that of a rushing storm. Frightened animals are fleeing before it in terror for their lives and birds are flying from the threatened destruction.

This scene passes, and now the whole visible earth is one vast stretch of coal black, and the whole sky is a thick blue haze in which the sun seems to hang like a great red ball, while an unbroken silence pervades the land.

Then winter comes with days of leaden sky and blackened earth, succeeded by clear days when the snow-covered earth appears like a vast white bowl encrusted with frost-diamonds and inclosed by an over-arching dome of most brilliant blue.

Again the season changes; warm airs blow from the south; soft showers fall; the sound of the first thunder wakens all Nature; the blackened earth appears once more, soon showing color from the pale green spears of tender young grass, and in a short time the form of Mother Earth is once more clothed in a mantle of shining green.

And now as the biting winds of winter yield to the balmy breezes from the south all the vernal flora is quickened into life and beauty. The modest blue violets appear in such profuse abundance that they seem like shreds of the sky wafted by the spring breezes over the land and drifted into every swale and ravine. On the upland the purple flowers of the buffalo pea show themselves; in sandy places of the Middle Great Plains the dainty lavender blue bonnets of the early wind-flower are trembling in the breeze. In the Northern Great Plains the snow is scarcely gone before the pasque flowers, first gladsome harbingers of the lovely hosts to follow, troop forth over the bleak hillsides, "very brave little flowers," the Cree Indians say, "which come while it is still so cold that they must come wearing their fur coats." This is in allusion to the furry appearance of the pasque flower.

And as the floral life manifests itself all the native faunal life is also awakened to renewed activity. The migratory birds are seen and heard flying northward by relays in hundreds of thousands. The course of the Missouri River marks upon the earth the chart by which they direct their northward flight toward their summer homing places. The Arkansas River, the Kansas, the Platte, the Niobrara and the White River are relay stations of their journey, and the countless V-shaped flocks coming northward in long lines wheel, circling down until tracts many acres in extent are whitened by the great numbers of snow geese, while the Canada geese in equal numbers darken other tracts; ducks in great numbers are swimming on all the ponds and quiet streams, and regiments and brigades of tall gray cranes are continually marching and counter-marching on land or sailing like fleets of monoplanes far up in the clear blue, whence float down to earth the vibrant notes of their bugle calls as they travel on into the North. On the higher prairies at sunrise as the long rays of the red morning sun slant brightly across the land the booming, drum-like sound of hundreds of prairie chickens is heard at their assemblies, for at this season they dance the mating dance at the sunrise hour. Soon the meadowlarks, "the birds of promise," appear, singing their songs of promise of good things for their friends, the human beings; and they set about the duties of housekeeping, building their lowly nests at the grass roots, and all about are scenes of brightness and sounds of gladness.

It was in such a country as this, then, that the people of the several different native nations who were here before us lived and took joy of the good gifts of Mother Earth and from their own activities, and in all the beauty of this good land. And they loved this land for all its good gifts and for its beauty, and for these and for its mystery and grandeur they paid reverence.

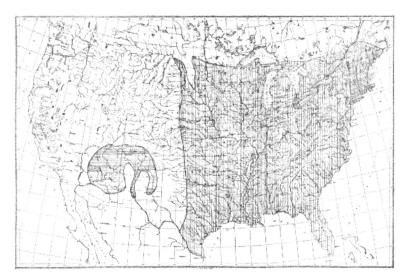

ABORIGINAL AMERICAN AGRICULTURE

See Map. Vertical lines indicate region under agriculture by natural rainfall. Horizontal lines indicate region farmed under irrigation. Both regions were settled in permanent villages.

Most people of this country, of the now dominant European race, seldom give a thought to the aboriginal economic conditions which prevailed here before this country was Europeanised. They seldom think of the precolumbian utilisation of the natural resources of this continent by the people of the native American race. They do not consider the myriad possible uses of plants and plant products by the people of the native tribes. Most persons of our European race in arrogant self-satisfaction have not been accustomed to think of those of the American race as agriculturists at all, much less have we given thought to the contributions made by that race to the world's agriculture. But according to the United States crop report of 1916 the value of the crops in this country alone, of plants which were first brought under cultivation by Indians, is $3,000,000,000.

No doubt the beginnings of agriculture, with our own European race and with every race, was simply the gathering and storing of supplies of wild plant products, and proceeded by the stages of intentional dissemination and cultivation, selection and improvement of stock into myriad varieties.

When European explorers first visited the Atlantic shores of America they found the native tribes to be agriculturists, living in villages of permanent houses, and with their cultivated fields stretching about the villages. And as the explorers advanced into the interior of the continent they found similar conditions to prevail as far as to and including the Missouri River valley. So it was found that in all the region from the Gulf of Mexico to the St. Lawrence River, the Great Lakes and the region of the upper Missouri river all the various Indian nations were settled agriculturists. On the High Plains and in the western mountains the tribes could not cultivate the soil because of the unfavorable conditions.

The crops cultivated by the tribes in the region above defined consisted of corn, beans, squashes and pumpkins in many varieties, gourds, sunflower, and tobacco. According to the testimony of some of the early explorers it appears that in the southeastern part of the continent they also cultivated sweet potatoes and peanuts. It may be said that the sunflower is native to the western plains and was there brought under cultivation and improved to what we have as the cultivated sunflower and was distributed throughout the region from the Great Plains to the Atlantic coast. The other crops above named were introduced from the south many centuries ago from Mexico. Their wild ancestors grow there, which would indicate that there they were first brought into domestication by cultivation and improvement of the wild stock. All evidence from every source seems to point to the plateau of southeast Mexico as the place of origin of corn. It seems to have been originally a large, coarse wild grass with seeds which were at least large enough to furnish an article of food when gathered in quantity. The botanical evidence would indicate that it was a branched stalk and that all the branches and the terminal alike bore loose panicles of seeds, not in compact ears as we now know the corn ear. But ages of cultivation and selection by obscure and forgotten tribes of primitive farmers have produced a plant which bears its staminate flowers generally on the terminal and its pistillate flowers on side branches modified into what we know as the corn ear. Not only had the above-described modification taken place in the process of long ages of cultivation and selection, but the five great types of corn had been formed and developed into innumerable varieties of each type prior to the advent of white men on this continent. The five types to which I have referred are dent corn, flour corn, flint corn, sweet corn, and pop corn. Dent corn was obtained first by white men from the Indians of Virginia in the beginning of the seventeenth century at the first settlement of that colony by the English. The New England tribes had flint corn, flour corn, and sweet corn, and pop corn, but not dent corn. The tribes of the upper Missouri River had flint corn, flour corn and sweet corn.

The Arikara and Mandan on the upper Missouri were the great agricultural tribes of this region. Omaha legend credits the Arikara with first having corn and with having distributed to other tribes. And the common pictograph to represent the Arikara among all the surrounding tribes was a conventionalised ear of corn. In the sign language also the surrounding tribes designated the Arikara by a motion of the hands depicting the act of shelling corn, or by the motions of eating an ear of corn. Washington Matthews says: "There are some reasons for believing that the Arikara represent an older race of farmers than the Mandan; for their religious ceremonies connected with the planting are the more numerous, and they honor the corn with a species of worship." And it is the work of these northern tribes in past centuries in acclimating corn to the short northern summer with its cool nights which has made it possible for the states of North Dakota, Montana and Minnesota now to be corn-producing states; for acclimation is a long and gradual process and was accomplished during a northward migration from Mexico which occupied many centuries of time.

In the arid region of what is now New Mexico and Arizona the work of agriculture was carried on by means of irrigation ages before the coming of white men, and the old irrigation ditches made by the primitive Indian farmers of that region may still be traced—irrigation works made without other power than human muscles and without the use of iron; the shovels used being made of bone.

The world is indebted to the aboriginal American agriculturists not only for all types of corn which we now have, but also for all kinds of beans, for pumpkins and squashes, cultivated sunflowers, sweet potatoes, peanuts, and many other crops among our present day staples.

A great handicap to the primitive American farmer was the lack of iron tools; for they had no iron before the coming of white men. Another handicap was the absence of horses. The horse was not native to the western hemisphere, and was first introduced by the Spaniards. Previously the only beast of burden in North America was the dog. So the cultivation of the ground was entirely handwork; and the tool most in use was a hoe made from the shoulderblade of the buffalo or of the elk. One may imagine the immense labor which was required to develop and extend the above-named crops over the continent, acclimated and ready to our hand when we arrived in the New World.

THE EARTH-LODGE

As an example of the modifying power of geographic influence exercised upon the arts, we may consider the style of architecture or domiciliary structure prevailing in the Plains region. In each geographic province, which also constitutes a culture area, the style of housing is different according to natural resources and climatic conditions. In the Plains area the permanent dwelling was the earth-covered structure; while the temporary dwelling was the skin tent.

The earth-covered house seems to be an evolution from the thatched house of the southern plains, exemplified in the dwellings of the Wichitas. Farther north the exigencies of the climate suggested the addition of an earth covering.

All the nations and tribes of the Missouri, of whatever racial stock, employed the same style of dwelling. In order to effect the construction of an earth-covered house, a circle of the desired diameter was stripped off from the surface soil. Four tall, strong forked posts were set in the center about 8 or 10 feet apart in a quadrangle. Beams were laid on these forks. Outside of the center posts a circle of shorter posts was set and beams laid in their forks. Rafters were laid from the lower to the upper beams. A wall of timbers was leaned up against the circle of lower beams, the base of the leaning timbers resting upon the ground. An opening was left at the east, and here was made a vestibule 6 to 14 feet long.

Timbers were laid upon the rafters, willow poles were laid upon the timbers, and a thatch of dry grass upon these poles. A covering of earth was now built up about the walls and over the roof to a total thickness of about 2 feet, making, when complete, a dome-shaped structure.

All structural timbers and poles were fastened by tying with ropes of raw hide or of basswood or elm fiber.

An opening of several feet in diameter was left at the top of the dome for a skylight, ventilator, and smoke-escape. The fireplace was at the center of the earth floor; the sleeping compartments were ranged about next to the wall. The altar was at the west side, opposite the doorway.

The diameter of the house varied, according to the needs of the family which occupied it, from 30 to 50 or 60 feet; the height from 15 to 20 feet. This was a family domicile and not a community or tenement house. Such family dwellings were clustered in villages. The evidences of many such village sites may be seen throughout all the region of the Missouri River drainage basin. Their fields of agricultural crops were cultivated in alluvial valleys usually near the villages, although sometimes, when suitable land was not nearby, their fields might be at some distance.

The earth-covered house probably originated with the tribes of Caddoan stock, that is, the Pawnee and Arikara, and was adopted by the tribes of other stocks upon their migration into the Missouri River region.

The Pawnee had very elaborate ceremonies and traditions connected with the earth-lodge. The earlier star cult is recognized in the signification attached to the four central posts. Each stood for a star—the Morning Star, and the Evening Star, symbols of the male and female cosmic forces, and the North and South stars.

In the rituals of the Pawnee the earth-lodge is made typical of man's abode on the earth; the floor is the plain, the wall the horizon, the dome the arching sky, the central opening the zenith, the dwelling-place of Tirawa, the invisible power which gives life to all creatures.

In the poetic thought of the Pawnee the earth was regarded as Mother and was so called because from the earth's bounty mankind is fed. To their imagination the form of the earth-lodge suggests the figure of speech by which these human dwellings symbolised the breasts of Mother Earth; for here man is nourished and nurtured, he is fed and sheltered and blessed with tenderness of life. Here he knows love and warmth and gentleness.

Herewith is given a metrical translation of an ancient Pawnee ritualistic hymn. This hymn is extracted from the ritual of a ceremonial of great age in the Pawnee nation, and there were similar ceremonials among all the tribes and nations of the Plains area. The full ritual from which this is taken is published in the Twenty-second Annual Report of the Bureau of American Ethnology, part 2.

Having given the description of the structure of the earth-lodge, the allusions in the following hymn will be readily understood:

HYMN TO THE SUN

I

Now behold: hither comes the ray of our father Sun; it cometh over all the land, passeth in the lodge, us to touch, and give us strength.

II

Now behold: where alights the ray of our father Sun; it touches lightly on the rim, the place above the fire, whence the smoke ascends on high.

III

Now behold: softly creeps the ray of our father Sun; now o'er the rim it creeps to us, climbs down within the lodge; climbing down, it comes to us.

IV

Now behold: nearer comes the ray of our father Sun; it reaches now the floor and moves within the open space, walking there, the lodge about.

V

Now behold where has passed the ray of our father Sun; around the lodge the ray has passed and left its blessing there, touching us, each one of us.

VI

Now behold: softly climbs the ray of our father Sun; it upward climbs, and o'er the rim it passes from the place whence the smoke ascends on high.

VII

Now behold on the hills the ray of our father Sun; it lingers there as loath to go, while all the plain is dark. Now has gone the ray from us.

VIII

Now behold: lost to us the ray of our father Sun; beyond our sight the ray has gone, returning to the place whence it came to bring us strength.

DESCRIPTION OF THE TIPI

The temporary dwelling used for traveling was a conical tent made from buffalo skins erected on a frame of poles. It commonly had about twenty poles averaging twenty-five feet in length. The poles were set in a circle about fifteen feet in diameter, held together above by a hide rope wound round the whole set of poles about four feet from the upper ends. Three poles were first tied together, then the others were laid in the forks of these, then the rope was passed round all of them and tied. The cover was from fifteen to eighteen buffalo hides cut and fitted so that when sewn together with sinew thread, they formed a single large sheet nearly semi-circular in shape. This was lifted into place by a special pole at the back of the structure, then the ends were brought around to the front and fastened by means of eight or ten small wooden pins at intervals from the door to the crossing of the poles. The bottom was kept in place by pegs about two feet apart around the circle. The door was usually a piece of skin stretched over an elliptical frame.

At the top an opening was left for ventilation and outlet for the smoke of the fire. The draft was regulated by two flaps or wings supported each on a movable pole slanted alongside the tipi with its base on the ground and its top fastened to the apex of the smoke-flap. This held the draft open to the side away from the wind and was moved according to the changes of the wind so as always to be open to the lee side.

The beds were at the sides and the back of the tipi. Decorated curtains above the beds kept off any drops of rain which might come through the smoke-hole in rainy weather. The ground was the floor, the part near the beds sometimes cut off from the open space by a hedge of interwoven twigs.

In warm weather the bottom of the tipi was raised to allow the breeze to pass through. In cold weather the bottom was banked with grass to keep out the wind.

The camp was arranged in a circle, each band of the tribe having its own proper segment of the circle, which was relatively the same through immemorial generations, and each family in each band had its proper place in the segment, so that one coming into camp after nightfall, although he might not have been in camp before, could thus unfailingly find his way to his own family.

On account of its exact adaptability to prairie life, the tipi was taken as the model of the army tent which bears the name of General Sibley, and is used now by our army.

AN OMAHA GHOST STORY

In the springtime a little child had died and was buried on the hill southeast of the village. The hill was green with the prairie grass and spangled with the beautiful wild flowers of the prairie. On the north and east the forest ascends the slope from the Missouri River valley to the crest of the hill, partly encircling the burial place with a rampart of green trees in which were numbers of happy birds, busy with their nest-building and tuneful with their joyful songs.

Not long after the death of this little child the people went upon the annual summer buffalo hunt to the Sand Hill region many miles away to the west from the village. As the people drew away from the familiar home scenes of the village the mother was strongly affected by a feeling of sadness and grief for her little one which she had to leave alone in its lone and narrow bed upon the hill. When the people made camp and the evening meal was prepared this mother was so burdened with grief for her child that she could not eat and went away to grieve alone. When she left the camp she was so drawn by yearning for her little one that she walked on and on all night toward the home village. In the morning, weak and weary, she was back in the deserted village. All was still. Not a person and not a dog was there. She went into her own house. Then she went through the village to other houses. At some deserted fireplace she happened to find some coals; so she was able to kindle a fire and cook a bit of food. She sat in her house and wailed for her baby. After a time she heard sounds. She listened and there seemed to be whispers and murmurs all about her. And so it continued day after day. At first she saw nothing, but heard the murmurs and whispers, and gradually she could almost understand what the whispers said, especially when she fasted. She made out enough to know that it was the spirits of the departed, who, in the absence of the living, returned to occupy the houses during the absence of the people.

After a time she became able to understand more of what the ghosts said, and finally she could talk with them in their own manner. Their speech was not like the speech of living people; there was no voice, but slight whispering sounds, as one sometimes hears among the grass on the prairie when all is still, or among the leaves of growing corn, or the light rustling of the cottonwood leaves on a quiet evening.

At first the woman saw nothing, though she could hear the whispering speech like the breathing of those who sleep. Later she could see, as it seemed, feet moving about on the floor, but nothing above the feet. As she looked she could see nothing between herself and the opposite walls of the house. Then, after a time, she seemed to see not only the moccasins but the leggings above them as far as the knees, but she never saw any more. And thus it was with her during all the time she dwelt there alone with the spirits until her people returned to the village.

This time it happened the people did not return for a year. When the woman had disappeared from the camp on their first night out the people supposed she had gone out somewhere to be alone to weep and pray, but when she did not return they sought for her, and not being able to find any trace of her they supposed some accident had befallen her and that she was dead. They were much surprised to find her at home when they returned to the village at the end of a year. But when they spoke to her they found that she was mute; she moved her lips, but no sound came. After some days she recovered speech and again took up her accustomed life with her people.

During the year in which she lived alone in the deserted village she had planted and harvested a crop and had lived by that and by what food may have been left in the storage places and from the wild products which she gathered.

AN OMAHA HERO SONG

All American tribes had many different classes of songs. One class of songs was in praise of tribal heroes. There were also songs of chivalry, celebrating brave and generous deeds. To this class belongs the one given herewith. It must be said in explanation that all Indian songs are very brief. They comprise only a line or two and the meaning of the song is known by the story which is its foundation. To understand this particular song it must be explained that a common military custom among the tribes was to award certain honors for certain exploits, just as we see in our own armies the awarding of the Victoria Cross, the Distinguished Service Medal, the Military Medal, the Croix de Guerre, etc. In the Omaha tribe the highest military honor was awarded for getting near enough to the enemy to touch an enemy body, either with a lance, a bow, or any object in the hand.

There was an old warrior of this tribe, named Yellow-wood Bow, who had fought well and won many honors in his time. But he was now old and no longer able to fight for his people. But one day when an attack had been made on his people by the enemy and the young men were fighting valorously, the old man went out walking feebly toward the field of conflict to see the battle, for he was unable to sit quietly in the village while the fighting was going on. It happened that as he approached the battlefield two young men were just about to count their honors by striking with a lance the body of a slain enemy when one saw the old warrior, Yellow-wood Bow approaching. He held back and spoke to his comrade in the words "Hold! Yellow-wood Bow is coming!" So the young men gave over the opportunity of counting the honor for themselves in order that the highly respected old warrior might have this one more chance to gain an honor, one more honor to his long list of honors. And the generosity of these two young men is praised in the song:

"Hold! Yellow-wood Bow is coming!"

In singing this song not only do the people award praise and glory to bravery and courage, but the virtue of renunciation shown by the young men also receives its measure of praise. The song has the purpose to inculcate emulation of bravery and also of generosity and unselfishness of spirit.

Stories of Plant People

SACRED TREES

A people living under natural conditions in communion with nature, will carefully note the appearance of natural objects in their environment. They become acquainted with the various aspects of the landscape and of the living things, plants and animals in their changes through the seasons, in storm and calm, in activity and in repose. Becoming thus intimately acquainted with the life about them the people will come to regard some of the more notable forms with a feeling akin to that which they have towards persons, and hence they come to have place in folk stories, in reasoned discourse and in ceremonies of religion.

Commonly throughout the region of the Missouri River was to be seen the cottonwood, the willows of several species, and the cedar or juniper. The appearance and habits of these trees impressed themselves powerfully upon the mind and imagination of the Indian folk.

The cedar or juniper was wonderful because it was ever green; unlike other trees it appeared indifferent to frost and to heat, but alike in winter and summer retained its leaves. Also it appeared to be withdrawn, solitary and silent, standing dark and still, like an Indian standing upon a hill with his robe drawn over his head in prayer and meditation. Thus it gave the suggestion, and had the appearance of being in communion with the High Powers.

Leaves and twigs of cedar were burned as incense in ceremonial rituals in order that evil influences might be driven away.

Willows were always found growing along watercourses, as though they had some duty or function in the world in connection with water, the element so immediately and constantly needful to man and to all other living things. Water was not only imperatively necessary for vivifying and reanimating all living things, but was an active agent in processes of change and transmutation. In cases of disease the evil influences which plagued the body might be driven out and thus health might be restored through the use of water transformed into vapor by means of heat. So the vapor bath was used. Also if a man contemplated the undertaking of any serious project, any dangerous mission, or any solemn enterprise, it was important first to prepare himself by purification, by means of the vapor bath, from all evil influences. The framework of the vapor bath lodge was made of willow poles, bent and tied with their bark.

The willow was also mystically connected with that greatest change of all, the departure of the spirit from the body, the change which we call death. Willow twigs had certain uses in funeral rites.

The cottonwood was found growing over a widely extended range, under diverse climatic conditions, appearing always self-reliant, showing prodigious fecundity, and having wonderful means of propagation. It provided its seed, produced in enormous number, with a device by which they traveled on the wind to far places and so became widely disseminated in all directions, traveling up-stream or down-stream, and even across the plains and prairies to other streams where the new generation might establish itself. But besides this admirable provision to insure the perpetuation of its kind it had also another means of propagation; though by this means it could move only down-stream. This method of propagation is by the making of cuttings or planting slips from its own twigs. It is well known that the gardener may make artificial cuttings of many kinds of trees and plants, and so increase his stock. But the cottonwood, alone among trees, performs this operation itself. At the beginning of autumn the cottonwood trees form layers of cork cells which gradually wedge off part of its twigs from the parent branch, thus covering and healing the wound of separation and also covering and healing the base of the separated twig so that it falls off alive and protected from loss of sap.

Falling thus to the ground just about the time that autumn rains are about to begin, they are ready to be carried away by the rising waters of the streams and may be thus planted in a mud or sand bank further down stream, ready to take root and grow in the springtime.

In the springtime the opening of the cottonwood buds and pushing out of the young leaves, even when chilly nights follow the bright breezy days and the rapid growth of these lustrous leaves, brightly dancing in the spring winds, their brilliant sheen and active movement reflecting the splendour of the sun like the dancing, glinting ripples of a lake, suggest the joy and eagerness and energy of movement of all returning life.

The foliage of the cottonwood is peculiar and remarkable so that it may be said the air is never so still that there is not motion of cottonwood leaves. Even in still and sultry summer afternoons, and at night when all else was still, ever they could hear the rustling of cottonwood leaves by the passage of little vagrant currents of air. Secret messages seemed ever to be passing in soft whispers among the cottonwood leaves. And the winds themselves are the bearers of the messages and commands of the Higher Powers, so there was constant reminder of the mystic character of this tree.

The cottonwood was, among trees, the symbol of fidelity, one of the four great virtues inculcated by the ethical code of the people of the Dakota nation.

So from all these considerations, it might be expected that this tree should have an important place in the rituals of the people for many generations associated with it. And so it had.

The Sacred Pole of the Omaha nation was made of the cottonwood. The Sacred Pole was an object of the greatest veneration to the people of that nation, similarly as the Ark of the Covenant was sacred to the Hebrew nation.

The Sacred Tree, the central object of the Sun Dance, the most momentous religious ritual of the Dakota nation, was a cottonwood. The tree which should be chosen to be felled and brought into camp and set up in the lodge erected for the performance of this ritual, must be a growing cottonwood tree, the base of whose trunk is not less than two spans in circumference. The tree must be straight and forked at a distance from the ground of about four times the measure of the outstretched arms from hand to hand.

Twigs and bark of cottonwood were burned as incense to ward against the scheming of Anog Ite, the spiteful malevolent being who foments scandals, strife and infidelity.

Such then, were some of the relations in the philosophic thought, the religious conceptions and the sentiments of the people of the Dakota nation in regard to these three species of trees.

THE SONG OF THE PASQUE FLOWER

The pasque flower (**Pulsatilla patens**), has a very extensive range upon the northern prairies, reaching from about latitude 43 degrees north to the Great Slave Lake above 60 degrees north latitude. It is the earliest flower to put forth its blossoms in the springtime, often appearing before all the snow is gone. Its bluish purple flowers gladden the bare brown hillsides with great profusion of bloom, in earnest of returning life. For this reason it has a strong hold upon the affections of all the native tribes throughout all its extended range. The plant is closely related to the anemone, which is sometimes called the wind flower.

The people of the Dakota nation have a number of pretty little folk stories concerning the pasque flower. One story is that in the long ago, whenever any of the people happened to pass by where these flowers were blooming they tried to show the friendliness which they felt for human beings by nodding their heads in the chilly spring wind, showing their smiling faces and saying, "Good morning! Good morning!" But the people passed them unheeding. They became abashed at this indifference, so nowadays still feeling friendly towards the people in spite of such rebuffs, they bashfully turn their heads to one side as they nod and call their kindly greetings in their sweet low voice.

There is another pretty conceit connected with the pasque flower. Indians generally are keenly observant of all things in nature, and reverent towards them. They feel reverence for all living creatures, whether plant or animal. They have songs and stories about most of the species of plants and animals with which they are acquainted, the specific song being the expression of the life or soul of the species to which it pertains. The song of the pasque flower, translated out of the Dakota language into English runs something like this:

"I wish to encourage the children of other flower nationsWhich are now appearing over all the land;So while they waken from sleep and rise from the bosomOf Mother Earth, I stand here old and gray-headed."

Map of Geographical Distribution of Pasque Flower

The saying: "I wish to encourage the children of other flower nations," refers to the very early prevernal blossoming of this plant and its consequent ripening while the other flower species (nations) are just peeping through the ground. The entire plant is hairy, and when mature its seed head is plumose and white, similar to the clematis head, suggesting the head of a very old man with long white hair. This explains the allusion in "I stand here old and gray-headed."

When in springtime an old man of the Dakota nation first finds one of these flowers it reminds him of his childhood, when he wandered over the hills at play as free from sorrow and care as the birds and the flowers. He sits down near the flower, upon the lap of Mother Earth, takes out his pipe and fills it with tobacco. Then he reverently holds the pipe towards the earth, then towards the sky, then towards the north, the east, the south and the west. After this act of silent invocation and thanksgiving, he smokes. Tobacco was sacred and was used ceremonially as an incense. The pipe was therefore a sort of censer, and was accordingly treated with respect and reverence. In smoking, Indians did not seize the pipestem in the teeth. Such an act would be sacrilegious. The mouthpiece of the pipestem was gently presented to the lips and the breath drawn through. By this inspiration the smoker united the mystery of the tobacco, the mystery of fire and the mystery of the breath of life.

While the old man sits by the flower and smokes he meditates upon all the changing scenes of his lifetime; his joys and sorrows, his youthful hopes, his accomplishments, his disappointments, and upon the guidance of the Unseen Powers accorded to him thus far upon the journey of life, and he is encouraged to believe that he will be guided to the end of life's journey "beyond the fourth hill" of life; as he has been guided over the hill of childhood, the hill of youth, and the hill of manhood's prime, that he will also be guided over the last hill, the hill of old age.

After finishing his pipe he empties the ashes reverently upon the ground near the pasque flower which he has been contemplating. Then he rises and plucks the flower prayerfully and carries it carefully home to show to his grandchildren, singing as he goes, the song of the pasque flower, which he learned as a child and which he now teaches to his grandchildren, commending to them the example of the flower in its courage and endurance and its faithfulness.

THE SONG OF THE PASQUE FLOWER

By Rev. Ignatius Forster, O. S. B.
Mount Marty, Yankton, South Dakota.
February 1, 1921.

Lovely Pasque Flower,Herald of Spring,Proclaiming the hour,Gladly to sing.

Gently thou greetestThe wintry sun;Boldly thou peepestIf snow is gone.

Callest thy playmatesWho still do sleep:"Arise, lo, spring waits!No longer weep."

Slowly they waken,Lowly they sigh:"Wasn't that beckonPasque Flower's cry?"

They rise in raimentsOf colors bright;Pasque Flower's garmentsAre hoary white.

Noble thy preaching,Pasque flower brave;"Work," is thy teaching,"Unto the grave."

Lovely Pasque Flower,Herald of SpringProclaiming the hourTo work and sing.

Father Forster was moved to write this delightful little song upon reading one evening, (February 1, 1921), the foregoing prose account of the Dakota (Sioux) Song of the Pasque Flower or Hoksi-Cekpa Wahca.

THE PRAIRIE ROSE

The prairie was gray and drab, no beautiful flowers brightened it, it had only dull greenish-gray herbs and grasses, and Mother Earth's heart was sad because her robe was lacking in beauty and brightness. Then the Holy Earth, our mother, sighed and said, "Ah, my robe is not beautiful, it is sombre and dull. I wish it might be bright and beautiful with flowers and splendid with color. I have many beautiful, sweet and dainty flowers in my heart. I wish to have them upon my robe. I wish to have upon my robe flowers blue like the clear sky in fair weather. I wish also to have flowers white like the pure snow of winter and like the high white cloudlets of a quiet summer day. I wish also to have brilliant yellow flowers like the splendor of the sun at noon of a summer day. And I wish to have delicate pink flowers like the color of the dawn light of a joyous day in springtime. I would also have flowers red like the clouds at evening when the sun is going down below the western edge of the world. All these beautiful flowers are in my heart, but I am sad when I look upon my old dull, gray and brown robe."

Then a sweet little pink flower said, "Do not grieve mother, I will go up upon your robe and beautify it." So the little pink flower came up from the heart of Mother Earth to be upon the sad prairie of her mother's robe.

Now when the Wind Demon saw the pink flower there he said, "Indeed she is pretty, but I will not have her trespassing in my playground." So the Wind Demon rushed at her shouting and roaring and blew out her life, but her spirit returned to the heart of Mother Earth.

And when the other flowers ventured, one after another to come out upon the prairie which was Mother Earth's robe, the Wind Demon destroyed them also and their spirits returned to the heart of Holy Mother Earth.

At last Prairie Rose offered to go and brighten the appearance of Mother Earth's robe, the prairie. Mother Earth said fondly, "Yes, dear, sweet child, I will let you go. You are so lovely and your breath is so sweet, it may be that the Wind Demon will be charmed by you, and that he will let you remain on his ground." And Prairie Rose said, "Yes, dear mother, I will go, for I desire that my mother's robe shall be beautiful. But if the Wind Demon should blow out my life my spirit shall return home to the heart of my mother."

So Prairie Rose made the toilsome journey up through the dark ground and came out upon the sad gray prairie. And as she was going Mother Earth said in her heart, "Oh, I hope the Wind Demon will allow her to live for I wish my robe to be beautiful!"

Now when the Wind Demon saw Prairie Rose he rushed at her shouting and said, "Indeed, though she is pretty I shall not allow her to be upon my ground. I will blow out her life." So he came on roaring and drawing his breath in strong gusts. Just then he caught the fragrance of the breath of Prairie Rose. "Ah," he said, "how sweet her breath is! Why, I do not have it in my heart to blow out the life of such a beautiful little maiden whose breath is so sweet! I love her. She shall stay here with me. And I must make my voice gentle and sing a melodious song, for I wish not to frighten her with my awful noise."

So he became quiet and breathed gentle breezes which passed over the prairie grasses whispering and humming little songs of gladness.

Then the other flowers also came up through the dark ground and out upon the dull, gray prairie and made it bright and joyous with their presence. And the wind came to love all the flowers and the grasses.

And so the robe of our Mother Earth became beautiful because of the loveliness and the sweet breath of the Prairie Rose.

Sometimes the Wind forgets his gentle songs and becomes loud and boisterous, but he does not harm a person whose robe is ornamented with the color of Prairie Rose.

THE SONG OF THE WILD ROSE

The following is a translation into English out of the Dakota language by Dr. A. McG. Beede, of an old Dakota song. The people of the Dakota nation, and other tribes also, think of the various plant and animal species as having each their own songs. With these people music, song, is an expression of the soul and not a mere artistic or artful exercise.

Where the word "Mother" appears in the following song it refers to "Mother Earth," a living, conscious, holy being in Indian thought. The earth was truly venerated and loved by these people, who considered themselves not as owners or potential owners of any part of the land, but as being owned by the land which gave them birth and which supplied their physical needs from her bounty and satisfied their love of the beautiful by the beauty of her face in the landscape.

The trilled musical syllables at the close of the last two stanzas express the spontaneous joy which comes to a person who has "life-appreciation of Holy Earth."

The first stanza is an introduction by the narrator; not a part of the "Song of the Wild Rose." The remaining stanzas are the song itself, of the Wild Rose.

I will tell you of something I know,And you can't half imagine how good;It's the song of wild roses that growIn the land the Dakota-folk love.

From the heart of the Mother we come,The kind Mother of Life and of All;And if ever you think she is dumb,You should know that flowers are her songs.

And all creatures that live are her songs,And all creatures that die are her songs,And the winds blowing by are her songs,And she wants you to sing all her songs.

Like the purple in Daydawn we come,And our hearts are so brimful of joyThat whene'er we're not singing we humTi-li-li-li-i, ta-la-la-loo, ta-la-la-loo!

When a maiden is ready to wedPin wild roses all over her dress,And a rose in the hair of her head;Put new moccasins onto her feet.

Then the heart of the Mother will giveHer the songs of her own heart to sing;And she'll sing all the moons she may live,Ti-li-li-li-i, ta-la-la-loo, ta-la-la-loo!

USE OF THE GROUND BEAN BY INDIANS

There is a native wild bean found growing over an area of wide distribution in North America. The botanical name of this bean is **Falcata comosa**. In the Dakota language it is called maka ta omnicha, which means "bean of the earth;" in the Pawnee language it is called ati-kuraru, which means "earth bean." The plant grows in dense masses over shrubbery and other vegetation in some places, especially along banks and at the edge of timber.

It forms two kinds of branches, bearing two forms of flower, producing two forms of fruits. Leafy branches climb up over the shrubbery, but under these, in the shade, prostrate on the earth, starting out from the base of the main stem, are leafless, colorless branches, forming a network on the surface of the ground. The tiny inconspicuous blossoms borne on these prostrate branches are self-pollinated and push into the leaf mold and soft soil, and there each produces a single large bean closely clothed by a thin filmy pod or husk. These beans which are formed in the earth are about the size of Lima beans. Upon the upper, leafy branches are borne showy, purplish flowers appearing like small bean blossoms. From these blossoms are produced small bean pods about a half inch to an inch in length. These pods contain each from three to four or five small, hard, mottled beans about an eighth of an inch long.

The large beans produced in the ground are desirable for food. They are of good flavor when cooked. The small beans of the upper branches are also good for food, but they are so small and difficult to harvest that not much use is made of them by the people. The large beans formed in the earth would also be hard to gather but for the help of certain little animals called voles, or wood mice, or bean mice. The voles dig the large beans and store them in considerable quantities in storage places which they hollow out in the ground and which they cover over with sticks and leaves and earth. In these places the little animals put away sometimes a peck or a half bushel of beans.

Through all the extensive range of **Falcata comosa**, the ground-bean, it was sought by the people of the various Indian tribes to add to their food supply. The people said they did not take away all the beans from the voles as it would be wicked to loot the animals' food stores and leave the animals to starve after they had worked to gather them. But they would take a part of the store, in a manner making themselves beggars to the little animals. The Omahas have a saying that "The bean mouse is a very industrious fellow, he even helps human beings."

But in all accounts I have had from the people of the Dakota nation the women have always said that they never took away any beans from the voles without making some payment in kind. They said it would be wicked and unjust to take the beans from the animals and give nothing in return. So they said they always put back some corn, some suet, or some other food material in exchange for the beans they took out. In that way they said both they and the little animals obtained a variety in their food supply. They said they thought it very wrong to deprive the animals of their store without such payment, but that it was fair if they gave a fair exchange.

The people of the Dakota nation speak of the wood-mice or voles by the designation of "Hintunka people." In the Dakota theory of the universe they personify the maternal power and spirit by the name Hunka. Hunka is the mystic All-Mother in nature, the mother of all living beings, plant or animal, which of course includes mankind. For they do not think of mankind as being apart from nature and the community of life in the world.

The Dakotas have a moral story which is told as follows:

A certain woman went and plundered the store-house of some Hintunka people. She robbed them of their entire food supply without even giving them anything at all in return. The next night this woman who had robbed the Hintunka people of all their food supply heard a woman down in the woods crying and saying "Oh, what will my poor children do?" It was the voice of one of the Hintunka women crying over her hungry children.

The same night the woman who had done the wrong had a dream. In her dreams Hunka appeared to her and said "You should not have taken the food from the Hintunka people. Take back the food to them, or else your own children shall cry for food."

The next morning the woman told her husband what Hunka had said to her. Her husband said "You would better do as Hunka tells you to do." But the woman was hard-hearted and perverse and would not restore to the Hintunka people the food of which she had robbed them, neither would she give them anything in exchange.

A short time after this a great prairie fire came, driven by a strong wind, and swept over the place where this unjust woman and her family were camping. The fire burned up her tipi and everything it contained, and they barely escaped with their lives. They had no food nor shelter and they had to wander on the prairie destitute.

The bean-mouse and its works are regarded with respect, admiration and reverence by the people of the various Indian tribes which benefit by its labor. They feel very resentful towards any seeming tendency to meddle unwarrantedly with its winter store-houses. Upon hearing of the desire of a white man to make a photograph of such a store-house an old man of the Teton-Dakota on the Standing Rock Reservation expressed bitter resentment and declared himself ready to fight to prevent such a thing from being done. He said "We have enough misfortune already, counting the war and the epidemic of influenza, without inviting further disaster by such sacrilege."

In the month of November, after the bean mice have harvested their beans and laid them up in their store-houses for the winter, the people often go out alone and sit near some such store-house in silent meditation on the ways of Providence. At that time of the year the missionaries and priests are often pained and puzzled because of the absence of some of their church members from Sunday service or from mass on Sunday morning. They do not know, and likely would not appreciate or understand the feeling which has caused these people to go out at such a time, not to the church but out to the quiet place under the open heaven where they sit upon the lap of Mother Earth to reverently and thankfully meditate upon the mysteries of nature and the wonderful provisions of God in nature.

At such times they like to bring in to their homes or to their churches some object connected with the bean mouse and his marvelous ways and work. If they find some beans which the bean mouse has spilled in transportation to his store-house, or a tree-leaf which they suppose he has used as his sled for carrying his beans from field to store-house, they will bring in such objects and lay them up reverently in the home or in the church with devout regard for prayerful meditation. Indians say that the bean mouse uses a leaf of the boxelder tree, or sometimes another kind of leaf of suitable shape, as a sled for gathering his stores.

At one time an old blind man of the Teton-Dakota on the Standing Rock Reservation on the upper Missouri River went out to the vicinity of a vole's store-house to meditate and pray. A man saw him and quietly approached within hearing distance. As the old man was blind he did not perceive the approach of the observer. Thinking himself alone in the presence of the powers of nature, this devout old man, gave expression to his religious feeling in the following prayer:

"Thou who art holy, pity me and help me I pray. Thou art small, but thou art sufficiently large for thy place in the world. And thou art sufficiently strong also for thy work, for Holy Wakantanka constantly strengthens thee. Thou art wise, for the wisdom of holiness is with Thee constantly.

"May I be wise in all my heart continually, for if an attitude of holy wisdom leads me on, then this shadow-troubled life shall come into constant light."

TIPSIN: AN IMPORTANT NATIVE FOOD PLANT

Over all the dry prairies of the Great Plains region there grows a plant (**Psoralea esculenta**), which was an important item of the food supplies of all the tribes of the region. It is a species which belongs botanically to the

Bean Family. The part used for food is the large root, which is stored with proteid and starchy matter. The root is about the size of a hen's egg. The stem of the plant is bushy and branched; the leaves are trifoliate. The leaves and stems of the plant are hairy, giving it a grayish-green appearance. The flowers are set in close racemes at the ends of the branches, and are bluish in color and of bean blossom shape.

In the journals of the early travellers mention of this plant is often found under the name of "pomme blanche" or "pomme de prairie," the name by which the French traders and trappers called it, for they learned to live upon the native products of the land. English speaking people coming later, and depending not so much on native products, did not supply names for them, not considering them of enough importance. The name which I have given it for a common English name is an approximation to, and an adaptation of the name of this plant in the Dakota language.

Tipsin roots are gathered in June or early July. They were used fresh when gathered, and they were also gathered in quantity and peeled and dried for future use. The women gathered them by the use of digging sticks. They had their children with them to look for the plants while they dug them. Because of the branching habit of the plant the mother would say to her children, "See, they point to each other. Now here is one, notice the directions in which its arms point and you will find others." So the children would start, each in the direction of one of the branches, and of course, if they followed in any direction and kept close watch they would find another. The idea of the plants pointing to each other kept the children's attention fixed.

HOW THE PEOPLE OBTAINED THE PRECIOUS GIFT OF CORN

All the tribes which cultivated corn had legends accounting for its acquisition. Many of these are very interesting and beautiful. In the Sacred Legends of the Omaha, of which account is given in "The Omaha Tribe," Twenty-seventh Annual Report of the Bureau of American Ethnology, by Alice Fletcher and Francis La Flesche, occurs the following legend of the finding of corn:

"Then a man in wandering about found some kernels, blue, and red, and white. He thought he had secured something of great value, so he concealed them in a mound. One day he thought he would go to see if they were safe. When he came to the mound he found it covered with stalks having ears bearing kernels of these colours. He took an ear of each kind and gave the rest to the people to experiment with. They tried it for food, found it good, and ever since have called it their life. As soon as the people found the corn good, they thought to make mounds like that in which the kernels had been hid. So they took the shoulder blade of an elk and built mounds like the first and buried the corn in them. So the corn grew and the people had abundant food."

While the legend does not designate what tribe it was which first obtained corn, it is probably to be identified with the following fuller account which is also told in the Omaha Sacred Legends, and which recites that they first learned of corn and obtained seed of it from the Arikara. The story tells how the Arikara first obtained corn by divine favour, and then how they gave it to other tribes, among these fortunate ones being the Omaha. It should be remembered that at the time the Omaha came to where they now reside and have resided for some centuries, the Arikara were in the region of what is now northern Nebraska, so they were then neighbors of the Omaha. No doubt the declaration of the legend that the Omahas did first obtain corn from the Arikara is based on fact, in that corn culture among the Omaha had been borrowed from the Arikara, who later migrated farther north along the upper Missouri River.

The story runs thus:

"The Arikara were the first to obtain the maize. A young man went out hunting. He came to a high hill, and, looking down upon a valley, he saw a buffalo bull standing in the middle of a bottom land lying between two rivers at their confluence. As the young man searched the surroundings to find how he might approach the buffalo he was impressed with the beauty of the landscape. The banks of the two rivers were low and well timbered. He observed that the buffalo stood facing north; he saw also that he could not approach from any side within bowshot. He thought that the only way to get a chance to shoot the buffalo would be to wait until the animal moved close to the banks of one of the rivers, or to the hills where there were ravines and shrubs. So the young man waited. The sun went down and the buffalo had not moved; the young man went home disappointed. He lay awake nearly all night brooding over his disappointment, for food had become scarce and the buffalo would have afforded a good supply. Before dawn the young man arose and hastened to the place where he had discovered the buffalo to see whether the animal might be somewhere near, if it had moved. Just as he reached the summit of the hill, where he was the day before, the sun arose, and he saw that the buffalo was in the same spot. But he noticed that it was now facing toward the east. Again the young man waited for the animal to move, but again the sun went down while the buffalo remained standing in the same spot. The hunter went home and passed another restless night. He started out again before dawn and came to the top of the hill just as the sun arose, and saw the buffalo in the same place still, but it had now turned to face the south. The young man waited and watched all day, but when darkness came he once more had to go away disappointed. He passed another sleepless night. His desire to secure game was mixed with curiosity to know why the buffalo should so persistently remain in that one spot without eating or drinking or lying down to rest. He rose upon the fourth morning before dawn, his mind occupied with this curiosity, and made haste to reach the hill to see if the buffalo still stood in the same place. Morning light had come when he arrived at the hill, and he saw that the buffalo was standing in exactly the same place, but had turned around to face the west. He was determined now to know what the animal would do, so he settled down to watch as he had throughout the three previous days. He now began to think that the animal was acting in this manner under the influence of some unseen power for some mysterious purpose, and that he, as well as the buffalo, was controlled by the same influence. Darkness again came upon him and the animal was still standing in the same position. The young man returned home, but he was kept awake all night by his thoughts and wondering what would come of this strange experience. He rose before dawn and hastened again to the mysterious scene. As he reached the summit of the hill dawn spread across all the land. Eagerly he looked. The buffalo was gone! But just where the buffalo had been standing there appeared something like a small bush. The young man now approached the spot with a feeling of curiosity and of awe, but also something of disappointment. As soon as he came near he saw that what had appeared from a distance like a small bush was a strange unknown plant. He looked upon the ground and saw the tracks of the buffalo; he observed that they turned from the north to the east, and to the south, and to the west; and in the centre there was but one buffalo track, and out of it had sprung this strange plant. He examined the ground all around the plant to find where the buffalo had left the place, but there were no other footprints except those he had already seen near the plant. He made haste to reach his home village. There he notified the chiefs and elders of his people concerning the strange experience which he had had. Led by the young man they proceeded to the place of the buffalo and examined the ground with care, and found that what he had told them was true. They found the tracks of the buffalo where he had stood and where he had turned, but could find no trace of his coming to the place nor of his going from it. Now while all these men believed that this plant had been given to the people in this mysterious manner by Wakanda for their use, still they were not sure what that use might be nor in what manner it should be used. The people knew of other plants that were useful for food, and the season for their ripening, and, believing that the fruit of this strange plant would ripen in its proper time, they arranged to guard and protect it carefully, awaiting with patience the time of its ripening and further revelation of its purpose.

"After a time a spike of flowers appeared at the top of the plant, but from their knowledge of other plants they knew that the blossom was but the flower and not the fruit. But while they watched this blossom, expecting it to develop into fruit, as they expected it would, a new growth appeared from the joints of the plant. They now gave special attention to the new growth. It grew larger, and finally something appeared at the top which looked like hair. This, in the course of time, turned from pale green to dark brown, and after much discussion the people concluded that this growth at the side of the plant was its fruit, and that it had ripened. Until this time no one had dared to approach within touch of the plant. Although they were anxious to know the uses to which the plant could be put, or for which it was intended, no one dared to touch it. While the people were assembled around the plant uncertain and undetermined how to approach the examination of it to learn its possible use, a youth stepped forward and spoke:

"'Every one knows how my life from childhood has been worse than useless, that my life among you has been more evil than good. Therefore since no one would regret, should any evil befall me, let me be the first to touch this plant and taste of its fruit, so that you may not suffer any harm and that you may learn if the plant possesses qualities which may be for our good.' When the people gave their assent the youth stepped forward and placed his hands over the top of the plant and brought them down by the sides of the plant to the roots in the manner of giving thanks and blessing. He then grasped the fruit, and, turning to the people, said, 'It is solid; it is ripe.' Very gently then he parted the husks at the top, and again turning to the people, he said, 'The fruit is red.' Then he took a few of the grains, showed them to the people, then ate them, and replaced the husks. The youth suffered no ill effects, and the people were convinced that this plant was given them for food. In the autumn, when the prairie grass had turned brown, the stalks and leaves of this plant turned brown also. The fruit was plucked and put away with carefulness. The next spring the kernels were divided among the people, four to each family. The people removed to the place where the strange plant had appeared, and there they built their huts along the banks of the two rivers. When the hills began to be green from the new prairie grass, the people planted the kernels of this strange plant, having first built mounds like the one out of which the first plant grew. To the great joy of the people the kernels sprouted and grew into strong healthy plants. Through the summer they grew and developed, and the fruit ripened as did that of the original plant. The fruit was gathered and some was eaten, and was found to be good. In gathering the fruit the people discovered that there were various colours—some ears were white and others were blue, some were red, others were yellow.

"The next season the people gathered a rich harvest of this new plant. In the autumn these people, the Arikara, sent invitations to a number of different tribes to come and visit them. Six tribes came; one of these was the Omaha. The Arikara were very generous in the distribution of the fruit of this new plant among their guests, and in this manner a knowledge of the plant came to the Omaha."

A GROUP OF PAWNEE HYMNS TO CORN

The Pawnee had migrated from the distant southwest into the Plains region, finally arriving at the region drained by the Republican, the Platte, and the Niobrara rivers. Corn was native in Mexico, and had been introduced into the Plains by gradual adaptation in cultivation along the line of migration of the Pawnee nation. These hymns express something of the high value which the people placed upon corn as an item of their daily sustenance. They also reflect something of the scenery of the Plains landscape. These hymns are from an ancient Pawnee ritual which is given entire in the Twenty-second Annual Report of the Bureau of American Ethnology, Part 2.

MOTHER CORN

I

Mother with the life-giving power now comes,Stepping out of far-distant days she comes,Days wherein to our fathers gave she food;As to them, so now unto us she gives,Thus she will to our children faithful be.Mother with the life-giving power now comes!

II

Mother with the life-giving power is here.Stepping out of far distant days she comes.Now she forward moves, leading as we walkToward the future, where blessings she will give,Gifts for which we have prayed granting to us.Mother with the life-giving power is here!

LEADERSHIP OF MOTHER CORN

I

The Mother leads and we follow on,Her devious pathway before us lies.She leads us as were our fathers ledDown through the ages.

II

The Mother leads and we follow on,Her pathway straight, where a stage each dayWe forward walk, as our fathers walkedDown through the ages.

The two preceding hymns reflect the fact that corn was introduced by the Pawnee from their more ancient homeland in the faraway southwest in remotely past time into the region of their later residence in the plains. They also reflect the importance which corn had in the everyday life of this people.

The following hymn to Mother Corn as Guide is expressive of the sense of vastness and awesomeness of the great extent of the Plains, and something of its grimness.

GUIDANCE OF MOTHER CORN

I

Looking o'er the prairie, naught our eyes discern there,Wide the land stretches out before us;Then we cry aloud to Mother Corn: "Doth thy pathway lie here?"

II

Heeding now our crying, while our eyes she opens,Mother Corn moveth out before usOn the lonely prairie, where we see straight the pathway lies there!

The following hymn of thanks for the corn shows something of the religious feeling of the Pawnee and their gratitude to Providence for the gift of corn.

A HYMN OF THANKS TO MOTHER CORN

I

See! The Mother Corn comes hither, making all hearts glad!Making all hearts glad!Give her thanks, she brings a blessing; now, behold! she is here!

II

Yonder Mother Corn is coming, coming unto us!Coming unto us!Peace and plenty she is bringing; now, behold! she is here!

THE FORGOTTEN EAR OF CORN

A woman of the Arikara tribe was harvesting her crop of corn, making ready to store it away in a safe place where she might be able to get it for use during the long cold winter. She went along gathering the ears and placing them in convenient heaps so that she could gather them up to carry to the storage place she had prepared. When she had finished her work she started to go, but she heard a voice like the voice of a little child, crying and calling pitifully: "Oh, do not leave me! Do not go away without me."

The woman was astonished at what she supposed was the voice of a lost child. She said to herself: "What is this? Can it be some child has wandered and has been lost in my cornfield? I must go and look for it."

So she laid down her burden of gathered corn, and went back into the field to make search. But she found no child anywhere in the field.

Then she started once more to take up her burden and leave the field. But again she heard the plaintive little voice crying: "Oh, do not leave me! Do not go away without me."

Then she went back into the field and searched again for a long time. After diligent search she found one little ear of corn which had been covered by stalks and leaves. It was the little ear of corn which had been crying, fearing to be left to die in the field. So all Indian women are very careful in gathering their crops so that nothing shall be lost or wasted of the good gifts of the Great Mystery, for they are accounted sacred and holy, and it would be wicked to treat them with neglect or indifference.

HOW THE USEFULNESS OF WILD RICE WAS DISCOVERED

A Chippewa Myth

Wenibozho and his grandmother, Nokomis, lived together in a lodge by themselves. When he approached manhood his grandmother exhorted him to exert himself, to learn to endure hardship, loneliness, cold and hunger and thirst, for such experience is the proper training for a young man. A young man needs such training so that when overtaken by misfortune he shall be brave and resourceful; so that he may be able to take care of himself and of any who may be dependent upon him.

So, one day Wenibozho told his grandmother he was going away into the wilderness where he had never been before, so that he could be cast upon his own resources to try his strength and courage and wit.

He was gone many days and nights, wandering through the forest and beside streams and lakes. He subsisted upon such fruits, seeds, roots and tubers as he was able to find, and upon the flesh of animals he was able to shoot with his bow and arrow which he had brought with him. One day he came to a lake in which was growing a great quantity of beautiful, feathery wild rice, swaying over the water in the gentle breeze. From the bark of a birch tree he fashioned a canoe in which he rowed out upon the lake and gathered a quantity of the wild rice. He did not know the wild rice was useful for food, for he had never seen it before, but he admired its beauty. He took the wild rice which he had gathered to his grandmother. He told her of the beautiful plant which he had found in the lake and that he had brought to her some of the seed of the plant. This seed they sowed in another lake near the place where he lived with his grandmother, for he hoped to have the beautiful plant growing where he might often enjoy its beauty.

Again he went away into the forest so that he might become accustomed to endure hardships and also that he might learn wisdom from the living creatures, not only from the moving creatures, but also from those other living creatures, the plants of all kinds. While walking he thought he heard a voice saying, "Sometimes they eat us." He stopped and listened and again he heard the words "Sometimes they eat us." This time he perceived that the words came from some bushes near which he was passing. Finally he spoke, saying, "To whom are you talking?" He was told that he was the one to whom the bush was speaking, so he dug up the plant and found that it had a long root. He tasted the root and it was pleasant to the taste, so he dug more, and ate a great many, so many that he was made ill. He was too ill to travel, so he lay there three days. Finally he was able to rise and move on, but he was hungry and weak. As he passed along other plants spoke to him, but he was afraid to eat of them. Then, as he was walking along a stream he saw some bunches of grass growing up out of the water which beckoned to him and said, "Sometimes they eat us." He was so hungry, and the graceful grass was so tempting, that he was constrained to gather some seeds of it and eat. The taste was pleasing, and its effect upon his hunger was so gratifying that he said, "O, you are indeed good! What are you called?" The Grass replied, "We are called manomin," which is the name which the Chippewa people call this plant. Wenibozho waded out into the water and gathered the grains by handfuls and ate it, and so continued till his hunger was fully satisfied. From eating the manomin he suffered no ill effects whatever, but was strengthened wonderfully. Finally he remembered the grain which he had discovered on his former journey and which he and his grandmother, Nokomis, had sown in the lake near their home. When he returned and found it growing and compared it with this grain which he had now found to be so good, he perceived that it was the same sort. So he found that this beautiful grass which he had growing in the lake near home was really manomin, as pleasant to the taste and as satisfying to hunger as it was beautiful to the eyes. Ever since that time the Chippewas have known how to value the good gift of manomin.

A STORY OF THE SUNFLOWER

A Story from the Dakota Nation

Once on a time, long ago, a company of men were going upon a war expedition. And now as they were within the country of the enemy they were proceeding very cautiously. One morning very early they heard what seemed to be the sound of someone singing in a tremulous voice, coming from the direction toward which they were marching. They stopped and stood still to listen.

As they stood thus listening it seemed to them that the singer, whoever he might be, must be a clown, for he was singing a clown song. There was not light enough to see the singer. But they waited silently and anxiously peering ahead in the direction from which came the sound of the singing. At the first glimmer of the dawn light they were able to make out the appearance of a man walking with an awkward shuffling gait. His robe was ragged and his leggings drooped down slouchingly in wrinkles about his ankles as he walked. He had great circles about his eyes painted a bright yellow and he was singing a clown song in a husky wheezy voice.

So they stood in wonder regarding the clown who was coming toward them. He was coming toward the sun rising and as the daylight grew brighter they were astonished to see the man suddenly changed to a sunflower.

And ever since that time, it is said, the sunflower is inclined to face toward the sun.

DAKOTA FOLKLORE OF THE SPIDERWORT

The spiderwort (**Tradescantia bracteata**) and (**Tradescantia occidentalis**) is a beautiful native prairie flower which is known under numerous popular names. It is called spiderwort, spider lily, ink flower, king's crown, and various other names. It has been proposed to add to the list another name, "flower-of-romance." This name is proposed from the circumstance of a bit of pleasing sentiment connected with this flower in the folklore of the Dakota nation of Indians.

It is a charmingly beautiful and delicate flower, deep blue in color, with a tender-bodied plant of graceful lines. There is no more appealingly beautiful flower on the western prairies than this one when it is sparkling with dewdrops in the first beams of the rising sun. There is about it a suggestion of purity, freshness and daintiness.

When a young man of the Dakota nation is in love, and walking alone on the prairie finds this flower blooming, he stops and sings to it a song in which he personifies it with the qualities of his sweetheart's personality as they are called to his mind by the appearance of the flower before him, its characteristics figuratively suggesting the characteristics of her whose image he carries romantically in his mind and heart. In his mind the beauties of the flower and the charms of the girl are mutually transmuted and flow together into one image.

The words of his song, translated from the Dakota language into the English, are something like this:

"Tiny, gladsome flower,So winsome and modest,Thou art dainty and sweet,For love of thee I'd die."

Stories of the Four-Footed People

THE FAITHFUL DOG

The dog was the companion and servant of the people over all parts of North America, and previous to the introduction of the horse into the western hemisphere by the Spaniards, the dog was the only domestic animal which the Indians had. After horses were introduced by the Spaniards, they soon came into use by the Indians, and in a comparatively short time they were widely spread over the continent.

But in former days the dog was the only beast of burden which the Indians had. They served as watchers at night, as companions and helpers in the chase, and as bearers of burdens in transportation service.

Once on a time a hunting party of men of the Dakota nation were in the buffalo grazing country in the time of the winter hunt. Scouts were sent out each day to look for a herd and to bring back report to the officers. One day one of the scouts discovered a herd near a certain lake. He came into camp in the evening, as soon as he could after he found the herd. At once he went according to the law and rendered his report to the proper officers. After reporting he went to his lodge and had his evening meal and then lay down to rest from the weariness of the day's scouting.

The officers held council and made the plans for the next day's activities of the hunting field. Then they sent the herald around the camp to announce the orders for the next day.

At the earliest light next morning every one in camp was up and making preparations for the day's work. It was yet early in the day when the hunters reached the lake where the scout had discovered the buffalo herd the previous day. Here they found the buffaloes still feeding. At the command of the officers the hunters and their dogs were deployed to surround the herd for the slaughter, for the meat supply of the people had become low, and at this opportunity they must replenish their provision.

The herd was feeding upon a strip of land which was surrounded on three sides by a lake. The plan was to advance upon the herd from the base of this strip of land and force them out into the lake where the huge animals would be at a disadvantage upon the slippery ice.

The men and dogs charged upon the herd and soon the great mass of shaggy beasts were forced out upon the treacherous ice where they were struggling in great confusion. Many were killed before the herd finally reached the shore of the lake and scrambled up the steep bank and fled away over the plain.

The sun was already past the middle of the sky and the hunters were busy with the work of skinning the carcasses and dressing the beef, making ready to carry back to camp their prize of meat, hides, and other useful products, when suddenly they saw and felt a great change in the sky and in the air. The threatening signs were evident of the swift approach of a blizzard, the dreadful and terrific winter storm of fierce, roaring wind and driving snow and frightful cold which frequently sweeps over the northern plains.

The hunters made haste to reach camp which had been made in the shelter of the woods not far away. Here a certain number had been detailed by the officers to make camp and to gather firewood, while the others had been taking care of the meat. Now as the fearful storm threatened, they gathered in the camp bringing in what they could carry of the meat supply. Soon the hunters were refreshing themselves with freshly broiled steaks which were much relished by the hungry men, who had eaten nothing since the early morning just before they had broken camp. The dogs too were given their share.

The storm was now upon them in its fury; and all about was a smothering, dizzying swirl of whiteness as impenetrable as the blackness of night. The gale of wind roared unceasingly; the myriad millions of tiny snow particles ground upon each other in the swirl of the storm, each infinitesimal impact adding to the aggregate of reverberation of sound, while the skin tents hummed like enormous drums.

From time to time those who were already in camp shouted to guide the later comers who gave answering shouts and came one after another staggering into camp exhausted by the buffeting of the storm. At last only one was missing. The herd scout, who had found and reported the herd the day before; he and his faithful dog had not yet come in. The fury of the storm throughout the night and the next day prevented the possibility of going to look for the missing man.

Toward morning following the second night of the storm its fury abated. As is usual, at the end of a blizzard, it was followed by an extraordinary calm. The drifted plain lay as still and white as marble. The stars glistened coldly like ice crystals in the sky. The air was so clear that the least sound made by any moving creature was magnified in the stillness.

The hunting camp awoke. Suddenly the game call of the great gray wolf was heard. And soon the hunters saw a great number of these gaunt gray creatures out upon the ice of the lake and on the plain, digging out the white mounds which were the snowdrifts about the carcasses of the buffaloes which the hunters had been obliged to leave when the storm came upon them.

And now among the wolf cries another sound was heard,—the defiant barking of a dog! It was the scout's dog. The men hurried toward the slaughter field to kill or drive away the wolves. Some wolves were dragging away a buffalo carcass, and from among the snarling howling pack about this carcass the hunters could distinctly hear the hoarse barking of their missing friend's dog, and occasionally they could hear a strangely muffled shout of a man sounding as though it came from under the ice.

The hunters finally reached the place to which the carcass had been dragged by the wolves. As the men came near the wolves ran away and the men saw the dog standing by the carcass for a moment before he fell dead as they reached the place. The men with their knives cut open the abdominal cavity of the carcass and found the missing scout inside wrapped in his robe in a bed of grass and buffalo hair.

When the storm had come upon him at his work he had seen that he could not reach the camp so he had opened two of the carcasses and removed the internal organs. In one he had made a bed for his dog, and in the other for himself for protection from the fury of the storm. The dog had kept an opening to his shelter, but the man had closed the entrance of his own after he was in, and the hide had frozen solid, making him a prisoner. When the wolves came the dog was able to free himself and tried to defend his imprisoned master, regardless of his own safety. He had been mortally wounded before the hunters could save him.

As soon as the scout was released he inquired for the dog, his friend and defender. When he saw that his loyal friend was dead, having given up his life in defense of his master, the scout was deeply moved with grief. He knelt down and stroked the head of the dead dog, and said, "Ah, my friend; you were courageous and faithful unto death. And you died like a brave warrior. You shall have the funeral of a dead warrior."

So with all due ceremony the scout carried the body of the dog to the top of a hill overlooking the lake where he had given up his life in doing his duty. There the scout laid the body. Over it he built up a tomb of boulders which he gathered from the hills. Then he laid upon it offerings of red paint and of food according to the funeral custom of his people, and they sang the farewell song for the dead.

Ever since that time this hill has been known to the Dakotas as the Grave of the Dog.

HOW COYOTE CHIEF WAS PUNISHED

A Mandan Story

Coyote Chief was out hunting one day, and he came upon a buffalo bull grazing. "Brother," he said, "you have nothing to do just now. Let us run a race to see which of us is the swifter." "All right," said the buffalo, "let us run."

"I shall first go and prepare a place for the race," Coyote Chief said, "then I shall come back for you."

So Coyote Chief found a high steep bank and placed on the very edge of it a small heap of stones. Then he returned to the buffalo and said, "Everything is now ready. Let us race over to yonder heap of stones which I have set up for a goal. When we are almost to the goal let us shut our eyes and run as hard as we can." And so they ran toward the heap of stones and the buffalo ran over the bank and was killed by falling, just as Coyote Chief had planned.

But Coyote Chief had nothing with which to skin the buffalo and cut up and prepare the meat. So he walked along a little way and came to a small clump of timber. As he approached the timber he called out, "Brothers, give me a knife." And they gave him a knife. Then he went on to another clump of timber. Here he called out, "Brothers, give me an earthen pot." And they gave him an earthen pot. He went on again to another clump of timber, where he called out, "Brothers, give me a horn spoon." And they gave him a horn spoon.

Then Coyote Chief went back to the place where the buffalo had fallen, and there he built a hunter's lodge of leafy branches of trees. Then he skinned the buffalo and pegged out the skin upon the ground and scraped it. Next he cut up the meat, and some of it he cut into strips and hung it up to dry.

Coyote Chief had Fox for a servant, to run errands and to work about the house. And he treated Fox badly and did not give him enough to eat. Fox was hungry, as usual, and tried to help himself to some of the buffalo meat, but Coyote Chief saw him and was angry. He seized a brand from the fire and thrust it into Fox's face, burning him thereby. Fox was hurt so badly that he decided to run away, but he wished first to be revenged upon Coyote Chief. So he went around to all the other animals and told them how badly he had been used by Coyote Chief. The animals were sorry for him and seemed willing to help him to punish Coyote Chief. So they held a meeting and talked over the matter to decide upon the best way to do this. The decision of the council was that they should all go over to his house that night and eat up all his meat while he was asleep.

Coyote Chief had worked hard all day to take care of his meat, and had not taken time to eat much. Being tired after his day's work he went to bed early. But he was anxious lest some one might come and take his meat while he slept, so before going to sleep he said, "Now my members, you must watch for me while I sleep. My eyes, if anyone peeps in you must stare hard at him. My ears, if you hear a sound, you must wiggle. My arms, if anyone comes in you must thrash around. My legs, if any one comes near, you must kick." Then he went to sleep.

That night all the animals gathered at Coyote Chief's house, but they were afraid to touch anything till they were sure he was sound asleep. So they sent Magpie first to peep in at the door. Magpie went and peeped in and saw Coyote Chief's eyes staring hard at him, and he went back and said, "He is not asleep, for his eyes stared at me."

After a time Crow was sent to find if Coyote Chief was not asleep. Crow flew up and perched by the smoke-hole. When he looked in Coyote Chief's ears began to wiggle. Crow went back and told the animals that Coyote Chief could not be asleep, for as soon as he looked in Coyote Chief's ears began to wiggle.

A little later Jack Rabbit was sent to look. Jack Rabbit pushed in a little at the door, and Coyote Chief's arms began to move up and down. So Jack Rabbit went back and reported that Coyote Chief must still be awake.

The animals again waited, and then sent Fox. Fox went inside, and then Coyote Chief's legs began to kick, so he ran out and told the others that Coyote Chief was still awake.

Now, after waiting quite a long time, the animals sent Mouse. Mouse went in and saw that Coyote Chief seemed to be sound asleep. He went up and ran over his legs and there was no motion; then he ran over his chest and still Coyote Chief was not disturbed. At last he ran over his face, and Coyote Chief did not stir. So Mouse went and told the others that Coyote Chief was surely asleep. Then they came in and ate up all the meat except a few scraps which dropped while they were eating. When they had finished eating they went away without having wakened Coyote Chief.

The next morning when Coyote Chief awoke, he was very hungry because he had eaten little the day before, and had worked hard; but he found his meat was all gone, and he said to himself, "Oh, why did I not eat the meat yesterday instead of waiting!" Then, because he was so hungry, he searched about on the ground and found some scraps of meat and some small bits of fat. All these he gathered up on a robe. He put fresh wood upon the fire, and then sat down by the fireplace with the robe over his knees to eat the little he had. But just then a spark shot out from the fire and lighted on his hand, which hurt him so that he jumped up suddenly, spilling into the fire all the shreds of meat and fat which he had so carefully gathered.

So Coyote Chief got none of his meat, and was punished for the bad way he had treated Fox.

THE SKUNK AND THE BEAR

A Mandan Story

One day a skunk was going somewhere, travelling quietly along a trail, thinking of his own affairs. He did not know it, but a bear was coming along the same trail towards him. Neither the bear nor the skunk knew that the other was on the trail until suddenly they met. They both stopped. Then the skunk said to the bear, "You are on my road. Turn out and let me pass!" The bear replied, "Not so. It is you who are on my road. Get out of my way!" But the skunk said, "You, yourself must turn aside." The bear then said, "Unless you do as I tell you I shall eat you at once. I tell you that you are on my road and must stand aside. I wonder how skunk meat would taste if I should eat some."

The skunk said, "I wonder how bear flesh would taste if I should eat some." Then suddenly the skunk threw up his brush and sprinkled the bear full in the face with his dreadful scent. The bear tumbled out of the path, howling in misery, and clawing at his nose and eyes. He could not see, and was almost suffocated.

As for the skunk, he passed on his way as if nothing had happened.

THE SONG OF THE OLD WOLF

There is a story told among the people of the Dakota nation that once on a time an old man went out, to be alone upon a high hill above the Missouri River to give himself to meditation and prayer. He chose this situation because of the grandeur and majesty of the view, of the great sweep of the prairie plains and hills, one hill beyond another away and away to the far horizon. Below flowed the wonderful and mysterious river, whose waters came down from the mighty mountains at the west and rolled on and on past the villages of many different nations, finally reaching the great salt water.

As the old man thus sat meditating and considering all the manifestations of life and power and mystery of earth and sky, he espied out upon the prairie a group of wolves trotting toward the river. When they reached the river they plunged in and swam across to the other side; all but one old one who was now too enfeebled by age to dare try his strength against the swift and powerful current of the river.

This old wolf sat down upon the bank of the river and watched his companions as they swam across and trotted away out of sight on the other side. When they had disappeared from sight he raised his muzzle towards the sky and mournfully sang in a man's voice the following song:

All o'er the earth I've roamed,I've journeyed far and wide;My spirit haste and go,I'm nothing, nothing now,I'm nothing, nothing now.

Missouri River, flow,Thou sacred water flow;My spirit haste and go,I'm nothing, nothing now,I'm nothing, nothing now.

After the old wolf had sung this song he wearily made his way to the top of a hill and lay down in the warm sunshine, in the shelter of a rock and there waited until his spirit went away.

And so now, when old men of the Dakota nation feel the infirmities of age creeping upon them, and as though they had been left behind in life's march, when they feel the depression of loneliness, will often go out alone to the summit of some high hill overlooking the Missouri River, and sitting there in solitude will muse upon their activities and noteworthy deeds in the past, of their companions of former days now long gone from them, and contrast all this with their present inactivity and loneliness. Then they will sadly and quaveringly sing this "Song of the Old Wolf."

Note.—The English translation and rendering into verse is the work of Dr. A. McG. Beede, of Fort Yates, North Dakota. The original song in the Dakota language is as follows:

Maka takomniTehan omawani;Minagi yayayo,Wana matakuni,Mni-shoshe yayoMni wakan yayo;Minagi yayayo,Wana matakuni,Wana matakuni,O he-he-he!

Stories of the People of the Air

FOLK SAYINGS ABOUT THE MEADOWLARK

The cheerful animation and lively manner of the meadowlark have made it a favourite with all people who are acquainted with it, both whites and Indians. And both whites and Indians attach words of their several languages to the notes of the bird. Among sayings in the English language attributed to the notes of the meadowlark are some expressions of banter and raillery. Farmers say that early in springtime the meadowlark perches jauntily upon the top of a fence-post and calls mockingly to them "You sowed your wheat too soon! You sowed your wheat too soon!" Another taunting expression fitted to the meadowlark's notes is addressed to girls and young women; it is "You think you're pretty, don't you?"

These locutions in English are in accord with the tone of many sayings ascribed to the notes of the meadowlark by the Hidatsa tribe of North Dakota, and with their name of the bird, **wia-akumakihishe**, which means "scolding or shrewish woman," for they say that the meadowlark says such taunting, tormenting and aggravating things. One of these taunting expressions is "**Kitho karishtiditore**," which is a most exasperating saying. **Kitho** means "that insignificant one," and **karishtiditore** means "good-for-nothing fellow."

The Omahas also put words of their language to the notes of the meadowlark. One of these is **Snite thingthi tegaze**, which means "winter will not come back." A little mixed-blood girl in the Omaha tribe was named Marguerite. Now the Omaha language does not contain the sound of the letter "r," so in trying to pronounce the foreign name of Marguerite they make it **Magathiche**. One day a friend of this little girl's father was at their house, and he was playfully teasing her because he was very fond of her. He said, of course speaking in the Omaha language, "Listen! do you hear that bird telling about you? He says: '**Magathiche hthitugthe!**'" The word **hthitugthe** in the Omaha language means "of a bad disposition," so her old friend was teasing her by putting words to the bird notes which meant "Marguerite is of a bad disposition," or "Marguerite is naughty!"

One of the sayings which the Pawnees fit to the notes of the meadowlark in their language is "**Kichikakikuridu!**" which means "I am not afraid!"

The meadowlark is a great favourite with the people of the Dakota nation. An old man of that nation was asked if his people ever used the meadowlark for food. He said they did not. When it was said that white men sometimes eat them, he said he knew that. Then, when asked why

Dakotas would not eat the meadowlark, he said, "We think too much of them. They are our friends." They call the meadowlark "the bird of promise," and "the bird of many gifts," for they say it promises good things to its friends, the Dakotas. They apply words of the Dakota language to the songs of the bird. They say it calls to the people with promises and with words of encouragement and good cheer, and that it gives counsel and advice on all manner of subjects. One of the things which it used to sing out to the people was "**Koda, pte kizhozho**," i. e., "Friends, I whistle for the buffalo," that is to say, it would whistle to call the buffalo in order that its friends, the Dakotas, might supply their needs of meat and clothing.

A touch of Dakota humour is shown in one saying attributed to the meadowlark's notes in these later times since the government has established schools on the reservations to teach the Dakota children in the ways of the white men. They say that ofter now the meadowlark is to be seen flitting about the school grounds and singing, "One, two, three, epedo! One, two, three, epedo!" The Dakota word **epedo** means "You shall say."

The white people speak of the United States government as "Uncle Sam," but the people of the Dakota nation call the government "**Tunkashila**," which means "Grandfather," a title of the highest respect. In the summer of 1918, while the United States was at war with Germany, many of the Dakotas said they heard "the bird of promise" singing "**Tunkashila ohiyelo!**" The Dakota word "ohiyelo" means "will be victorious" or "will have the victory;" so the meadowlark, "the bird of promise," was singing to them "The United States will have the victory!"

HOW THE MEADOWLARK WON THE RACE

A young man named Piya had a beautiful and lovely young wife and she was carried away by an evil monster who kept her hidden in his dwelling. The young man's grandmother was a very wise old woman. She had great knowledge of the birds and beasts and of the trees and other plants, and she had mysterious powers and could do many wonderful things. Also she had taught her grandson many things, so that he too had uncommon knowledge and powers.

Now when the monster stole his wife away he came to his grandmother to ask her to help him recover his wife. Before he came to her his grandmother knew he was in trouble, so when he came he found her waiting for him. She said "I will prepare you for this quest; but first bring to me a wolf, a turtle and a meadowlark." Then she brought him food; and after he had eaten and rested he set out to find the wolf, the turtle and the meadowlark. As he journeyed he found all of them, one after another, and invited them to eat with him. Then he told of his grandmother's wish to have them to aid him in his quest. They each consented to help him

- 73 -

provided the old woman would give him the thing most desired. The wolf said he wished to have a better fur coat so that the cold breath of old Waziya, the Old Man Winter, would not chill him. The turtle said, "Insects bite me, but I will help you if I shall be given protection from insects which suck my blood." The meadowlark said "My voice is harsh and I can sing but one note and the magpie laughs at me. I will help you if I may be given a pleasing voice so that I can make the magpie ashamed." So the young man Piya, the wizard, together with his three friends, the wolf, the turtle and the meadowlark came back to the tipi of his grandmother.

She was waiting and expecting him, and said, "Grandson I knew you would come and bring with you those whom I want." She invited them into her tipi and prepared food and set it before them. The next morning Piya told his grandmother that these friends he had brought had promised to help him if they should each be given what he most desired. Then she told them if they would help her grandson she would give each one what he most wished. So they were all agreed. She told the wolf she wished him to give her grandson the cunning by which he could follow a hidden trail and find hidden things; she asked the turtle to give him the sense by which he could locate water, so that he should be able to avoid perishing of thirst in a desert land; and the lark was to give him power to hide himself without covering in the open prairie. In return for these gifts the wolf was to have for himself and all his people warm fur clothing so that they could laugh at Waziya when he would blow his cold breath upon them. The turtle was promised that he should have the hard tough covering which he asked, so that insects could not bite him. The meadowlark was given a pleasing voice so that his songs would make the magpie ashamed.

After the agreement was made the Old Woman told them that the quest on which they had to go would take them into a country where there would be no trees, nor much grass nor open trail, and but little water in the hidden springs.

So the wizard, Piya, and his companions, the wolf, the turtle and the meadowlark set out upon the quest after the Old Woman had instructed them. The wolf taught him how to find hidden trails; the meadowlark taught him how to be hidden without covering, and the turtle taught him how to find hidden watersprings.

So the help of these friends, together with the powers he already possessed, enabled Piya finally to discover where his wife was hidden by the monster, and to rescue her.

So they all came back to the tipi of the Old Woman. They all rejoiced; the young woman because she had been rescued from the power of the monster; the young man Piya because he had found his wife; and the wolf, the turtle and the meadowlark because they were to have the gifts which they had most desired. The Old Woman prepared a feast and they feasted until far into the night.

Next morning the Old Woman gave to the wolf, the turtle and the meadowlark each the gift for which he had asked as a reward for helping the young man, and they set out together on the trail to return to their homes. As they journeyed they talked about the gifts which they had received. As they talked they fell into argument, each claiming that his gift was the best, and soon they were quarreling and were about to fight. But just then a young man came along the trail and he asked them why they were quarreling. They told him. He said that quarreling was foolish and would decide nothing, but that the only way to determine whose gift was the best was to find out which would help most in a trial of skill. The wolf proposed a trial in hunting, but the meadowlark and the turtle said they could not hunt. The turtle proposed a swimming contest, but the wolf and the meadowlark said they could not swim. Then the meadowlark in his turn proposed a contest in singing, for he was very proud of his gift, but the wolf and the turtle protested that they could not sing.

The young man suggested that they run a race. To this they all agreed. The young man told them they must run past a plum thicket, across a marsh and up to the top of a certain hill. There they would find white clay and colored clay. The winner of the race would be the one that first brought back to him some of the white clay. They set out upon the race. The wolf and turtle were running side by side; but the meadowlark fell far behind.

When he came near the plum thicket he saw a bundle laid up in the forks of a plum bush. He paused and sniffed toward it and the scent of it was strange to him, and he became curious about it, and wanted to find out what was in the bundle. He asked the turtle to wait. The turtle said he would wait for him at the marsh. The wolf walked all round the bush and looked carefully at the bundle. Then he rose up against the bush and sniffed at the bundle, but still he could not make out what was in it. He could not quite reach the bundle, so he leaped to try to pull it down. But as he did so the thorns pricked him. He jumped again and missed the bundle, but was pricked again by the thorns. Now he became angry and determined he would get the bundle. After jumping many times and being always pricked by the thorns so that he had many wounds on his sides and back he finally pulled down the bundle. He was so angry that in his vexation he energetically shook it about so that it was shaken open and its contents smeared his wounds. This made his wounds itch so severely that he had to scratch himself, but this made him itch the more. He was in such torment that he scratched madly and tore his fur coat and was bleeding, so he forgot the race.

The turtle ran on to the marsh and waited there as he had promised. After he had waited a long time he concluded the wolf had deceived him and had gone on to the hill. Then he saw a small white puffball. It looked like a lump of white clay, so the thought came to him that he could deceive the young man with it and get even with the wolf for the trick he supposed the wolf had played upon him. So he took the puffball back and showed it to the young man. Neither the meadowlark nor the wolf had returned yet, so the young man told the turtle he was the first to return bringing something to show that he had been to the top of the hill.

Now when the meadowlark ran by the plum thicket he saw the wolf jumping about one of the bushes trying to reach something which was there, so the meadowlark was encouraged to think he might still have some chance in the race. He ran on to the marsh, and there he saw the turtle waiting, so he was still more encouraged. He then ran on all the way to the top of the hill. He was so anxious and flustered when he reached there that instead of the white clay which the young man had specified as the token of having been to the goal, he made a mistake and picked up a lump of the yellow clay and turned to carry it back to the young man. As he was crossing back over the marsh again he stumbled and dropped the lump of clay into the black mud. He picked it up and hurried on, not stopping to clean off the black mud. When he came near to the young man he saw the turtle sitting there and smiling and looking very satisfied. The meadowlark then thought he had lost the race. He was so disappointed and discouraged that he wept. His tears washed the black mud off from the lump of clay and made a black stripe, while the yellow clay itself was washed down over the whole front of his clothes.

At last the wolf came back scratching and howling in his misery. Great patches of fur were torn from his clothes and his skin was raw and sore. The turtle taunted the wolf for his crying. He swaggered about and boasted that nothing could make him whimper and cry. The young man said that the turtle was the first to return, but that he must make good his boast that nothing could make him whimper if he should lose. The turtle declared that he would prove all he said in any way the young man should require. The young man then placed the puffball upon the turtle's back. The puffball very quickly increased in size and weight so that it was all the turtle could bear. It continued to increase in size until the turtle was borne down by it to the ground and his legs were bent. Still the puffball continued to grow until the turtle's body was pressed flat by it, and his breath was pressed out of his body and he lay as if he were dead. Then the puffball became as light as a feather and turned black. The turtle recovered his breath a little, but he was unable to straighten his legs or to regain the form of his body, so he was ashamed and drew in his head under his thick skin.

Then the young man laughed loud and long at the plight of the wolf, the turtle and the meadowlark, and told them now who he really was. He told them that he was Iktomi, the Trickster. He told them that because they had foolishly quarreled about the good gifts which the Old Woman had given to them, instead of making good use of them, they had given him the opportunity to play this trick upon them, the marks of which would be upon them, and upon their people forever. He said that because the wolf had meddled with something which was none of his affair he had brought upon himself the torments of the mange, and so it would always be with his people whenever they should do as he had done. He said that because the turtle had attempted to win by cheating, his legs and the legs of all his people should always be short and bent and their bodies should be flattened, so they could never run in a race. And because he had lied in saying the puffball was white clay, therefore he and his people should never again be able to speak, and they should always hide their heads for shame. As for the meadowlark, the young man said he had won the race, but because he had brought back the yellow clay instead of the white, therefore his clothes and the clothes of his people should always be yellow in front and there should be a black stripe over the yellow.

INDIAN FOLKLORE OF THE HORNED LARK

The name of this little bird in the Dakota language is **ishtaniche-tanka** (big eye-tufts) from the tuft of feathers which it has over each eye. It is for the same reason that we call it "horned" lark.

The Dakotas say that this little bird foretells the weather. They say that when a hot dry time is coming in the summer the bird sounds a single sharp little note; but when rain is coming the bird is glad and continuously sings loudly and joyously, "**magazhu, magazhu, magazhu!**" In the Dakota language the word for rain is **magazhu**. Thus the bird is singing its joy for the rain which is coming.

The name of this bird is **hupa-hishe** in the Hidatsa language. In that language the word for moccasin is **hupa**, and the word **hishe** means wrinkled. This bird is called "wrinkled moccasin" because of its appearance in its characteristic habit of crouching upon the ground, where, by its grayish-brown color and its black markings it is made inconspicuous and hardly distinguishable, suggesting the appearance of a ragged, useless old moccasin.

The Hidatsas have a story of this bird that it was once acting as a spy in enemy country. So while it sat in its characteristic attitude of inconspicuousness, two of the enemy were coming along, when one thought he saw something. He stopped and said to his companion, "Wait, what is that over there?" His companion glanced over and saw what appeared to him like nothing but a ragged, rotten old fragment of a worn out moccasin, and answered, "O, that is just an old wrinkled moccasin." So the bird escaped his enemies, and it is from that that the people call him "hupa-hishe."

HOW IT CAME ABOUT THAT GEESE MIGRATE

The Teton-Dakota have a story which says that "Long, long time ago" (lila ehanna) the goose nation did not migrate to the south in the autumn, but remained here throughout the winter time. Because of the rigor of the winter most of the people of the goose nation perished so that they were always a small and weak nation. At last one goose had a dream of the south-land, that it was pleasant even in winter, that the winter there was mild and that there was plenty of food there. So she began teaching the other geese that they should practice flying more and thus make their wings strong so they could fly to the south-land before winter time. Some people of the goose nation believed the vision and began to practice flying to make their wings strong for the autumn journey. This caused discussion and dissension in the nation, and a law was made which banished the goose which had the vision. So they drove her out from among them. She practiced flying all summer and made her wings strong so that in the autumn she was able to fly to the pleasant south-land of which she had dreamed. The Mysterious Power which had given her the vision guided her on the long journey and she lived pleasantly through the winter time. After the first thunder in the springtime she flew back north to her nation. As always before, many of them had died during the cold winter-time from the fury of the storms and the scarcity of food. But she told them how pleasantly she had passed the time in the south-land, and they saw in what good health she was, so many more of them now believed her vision and her teaching. It was in this way that the geese learned to fly away to the south-land in the autumn to escape the storms and cold of winter in this land.

THE CAPTIVE BIRD: A TRUE STORY OF CHILDHOOD IN THE OMAHA TRIBE OF NEBRASKA

Indians in general have a close sympathy with nature and with all living creatures and aspects of nature. And the term living creatures includes plants as well as animals, all are living children of Mother Earth and have their rights to life according to Indian thought. They do not think of humankind as being above and separate from all other creatures, but as fellow creatures in a world of life.

The following incident, which took place about fifty years ago on the prairies of Nebraska among a group of children of the Omaha tribe, will serve to show the attitude quite commonly held by Indians toward other forms of life. It might be well, also to mention in this connection that Indian children were taught by their parents to be not wasteful and destructive of wild flowers, that they should not wantonly pluck them, for, they were told, if they did so they would thus destroy the flower babies and the flower nations would then be exterminated. Indians feel a fearful dread of the consequences of interfering with the nice balance and adjustment of nature.

It was a bright, warm summer afternoon in northern Nebraska. The wild grass, waving in the summer breeze, was like a shimmering emerald sea, flecked with varied colour of the many different tribes of wild flowers. Overhead was a brilliantly blue sky with here and there slow-sailing white clouds whose soft shadows came and passed, silent and entrancing, over the greenth of the prairie. And in all this scene the living creatures were moving, intent upon affairs of their own; the crickets and grasshoppers, and the small mammals among the grass, the butterfly flitting from flower to flower, the antelope grazing in groups, and now and then a hawk might be seen circling high overhead.

Across the prairie came a caravan of people with their camp equipage. A band of Omahas was on the summer buffalo hunt. The men were widely deployed in front and over a wide extent on both sides far in advance of the moving column. They were on the lookout for signs of the herd. When a herd should be sighted, the scouts who had found them would at once report to the officers. When the camp was made the officers would confer and make plans for the surround and kill.

The boys were employed in looking after the herd of extra horses; some of the women were with the train of pack animals looking after the baggage and camp equipment, others were scattered over the prairie along the line of march, carrying digging sticks and bags to gather tipsin roots for food.

Groups of small children, too small to have any particular tasks assigned to them were playing along the way, observing the ways of beast and bird and of insects, and admiring the brilliant wild flowers. One such group found a fledgling meadowlark, not yet able to fly. They captured it and brought it along with them when the band went into camp for the night. As the families sat about their tents waiting the preparation of the evening meal, the children showed their father the captive bird and told him how they caught it. He listened to their account and then told them something of the life and habits of the bird, its nesting and home life, of its love of life and freedom, and of its place in the world under the wise plans of the Master of Life. He brought the children to see the unhappiness and the terror which they had unwittingly brought upon the captive and the anxiety the mother bird would feel over its loss.

Then he said to them, "Now children, take the little bird back to the place where you found it and set it down in the grass, and say 'O Master of Life, here is thy little bird which we have set free again. We are sorry that we took it away from its home and its people. We did not think of the sorrow we should cause. We wish to restore it and have it happy again with its people. May we be forgiven for our thoughtlessness and we will not do such wrong again.'"

The children carried out their father's instructions and placed the little bird again as near as they could to the place where they had captured it and recited the prayer to the Master of Life which their father had admonished them to say. As they returned to the camp the quiet of the summer evening lay over all the land, the after-glow of the sunset was in the western sky, the white tents stood in a great circle upon the prairie, now dusky-green in the twilight which lay upon the land, a twinkling camp-fire before each tent. The children were thoughtful. They had had a glimpse of the unity of the universe. They never forgot the lesson. Years passed, great changes came. The white people were coming into the land. Old activities and industries of the Indians were destroyed by the changes. The children of that little group went away from their people to attend the white men's schools, to learn the white men's ways and adapt themselves to those ways. But this did not cause them to forget altogether the wisdom and grace of their parental teaching. Long afterward they told this little story to the writer, who now gives it to you, reader, and wishes that you, also may know that there be those in all lands and among all peoples who "do justice, love kindness, and walk humbly with God."

THE CHICKADEE

The chickadee is a very popular bird among all the Indian tribes where it is known. They all have many stories and sayings about it. They say of it that, though small, it is a very wise bird. It is like the wise men, the doctors and teachers among the people, who are learned in mysteries and the wonderful things of nature, who keep a calendar of the cycle of the days, months and seasons through the year by cutting marks upon a piece of wood which they have prepared for that purpose.

This wise little bird is said also to keep account of the months. It is said that "in the beginning" the task of keeping account of the months was assigned to the chickadee. But instead of making notches in a piece of wood as the wise men do this wise bird's method is to make notches in its tongue; thus in September its tongue is single-pointed, in October it has two points, in November three, and so on until February, when it is said that its tongue has six points. Then in March its tongue is again single-pointed and the count is begun again. So, it is said, the chickadee has been keeping the count of the months since the long ago, in the dim past, when the task was assigned to it in the time of beginnings, in the time when evil powers and monsters struggled mightily to overcome the good, and to destroy mankind by sending fierce storms and heavy snowfalls and shuddering cold winds upon the face of the earth. It was thus the evil powers sought to discourage and to overcome mankind.

And so it is said that at one time the evil powers supposed that by stress of a long siege of cold and storms they had reduced mankind to famine. At this time they chose to send the chickadee as a messenger to find out the conditions and to bring back word to them.

Now when the chickadee came on his mission and appeared at the dwellings of men he was invited to enter. He was courteously given a place by the fireside to rest and warm himself. Then food was brought to him. After he had eaten and refreshed himself he was anointed with fat, which was a symbol of plenty; then he was painted with red paint, which was for a symbol of the power and mystery of life. After these ceremonies and marks of respect his hosts quietly composed themselves to give attention to whatever their visitor should have to say as to the purpose of his visit. When he had stated his mission his hosts held counsel and formulated a reply for the messenger to take back to those who had sent him. He was bidden to say to them that mankind was still living and hopeful, and they ever would be; that they could not be daunted by discouragement, nor defeated by storms and stress, nor vanquished by hunger, nor overcome by any hardships; and that there never would be a time when there should not be men upon the earth. So this is the message which the chickadee brought to the evil powers which had sought to overcome mankind.

THE SONG OF THE WREN

A Pawnee Story

The incident of this story occurred in the long ago in the country of the Pawnee nation, in the broad expanse of the Platte River country in what is now the State of Nebraska. The event was in the distant past before the Pawnees had ever seen a white man, or any of his works or strange devices. The people of the Pawnee nation lived in villages of houses built in the manner that the houses of Pawnees had been built for generations. Near their villages lay their fields of corn and other crops which they cultivated to supply themselves with food.

It was a beautiful morning in early summer. The sky was clear and bright, the dawn-light was showing in the eastern sky. All the landscape lay as though still sleeping. There was no movement anywhere. A thoughtful priest had risen and had walked out upon the prairie away from the village so that he might view and meditate upon the beauty and mystery of the firmament of the heavens and of the plane of earth, and of the living creatures thereon, both animal creatures and plant creatures, for in his mind both were equally wonderful and equally interesting, as showing the power and the wisdom of the Great Mystery. So he walked and pondered upon all the beauty and mystery which lay about him, while the face of Mother Earth was still moist with the dew of sleep. In a moment the first rays of the sun shone across the land touching into sparkling brilliance the myriads of dewdrops, while a gentle movement ran through all the grasses and the wild flowers as they swayed to the rippling of the gentle morning breeze which pulsed over the prairie at the first touch of the morning gleam.

Where a moment before all had been so still and so silent now there was movement and sound. Birds of many kinds raised their tuneful voices, showing their joy in life and in the beauty of the morning. The priest, whose mind and heart were open to all this beauty and melody, stood still and listened. In a moment, among all the other bird-songs, he heard one which was clearer and more remarkable than any of the others. This song was a most joyous cheerful sound, like happy laughter. As he approached he found that the joyous, laughing song came from a very tiny brown bird, no larger than his thumb. It was a wren, so small, so insignificant in comparison to the size and brilliant plumage of many of the other birds, yet it appeared to be the most whole hearted in joy and praise and delight in life, as the sweet stream of music welled from its little throat.

The priest looked at the tiny bird, and wisely considered. He said to himself: "The Great Mystery has shown me here a wise teaching for my people. This bird is small and weak, but it has its proper place in the world of life and it rejoices in it and gives thanks with gladness. Everyone can be happy, for happiness is not from without, but from within, in properly fitting and fulfilling each his own place. The humblest can have a song of thanks in his own heart."

So he made a song and a story to be sung in a great religious ritual of his people, which was to them like our Bible and prayer-book are to us. And the song and story which that thoughtful priest put into the ritual, was the story of the wren. And ever since that time so long ago, the song has been sung by the Pawnees and has been handed down from generation to generation until this time.

THE WAR EAGLE AND THE JACK-RABBIT

A Mandan Story

One time a party of men went into a lonely place among the hills far away from the village, to enter their eagle pits for the purpose of catching eagles to obtain their plumes. One of the men had made his pit far out at some distance from any of the others. Another day, as he was coming away from his eagle pit, returning to the village, he stopped and sat down upon the top of a high hill from which he could enjoy a grand view of the landscape. Thus he sat looking about over the quiet hills and valleys, beyond the bright gleam which showed the course of the river winding in and out among the green trees along its borders, far away to the dim sky line. Far away on one side he saw a number of elks feeding; on the other side he saw a band of graceful antelopes. A doe and her fawn were browsing upon some bushes down near the river.

Aloft he saw the white clouds sailing in the bright blue sky; below he saw their shadows moving over the earth, now up a hillside and over its crest and then swiftly across a little valley and up the next hillside. While he sat enjoying the beauty of the scene he observed a war eagle chasing a jack-rabbit. The jack-rabbit continually dodged and circled, trying to escape as the eagle swooped toward him. The eagle had several times swooped and just missed striking the rabbit.

Gradually the chase came near to the place where the man was seated. The eagle was closely pursuing the rabbit and made a tremendous swoop towards him. But the rabbit escaped by leaping into the man's robe as he sat with it loosely draped about his shoulders and knees.

Then the eagle said "Put that rabbit away from you! He is my prey. I intend to eat him."

But now the rabbit appealed to the man and said, "I have thrown myself upon your kindness. Do not turn me away. I beg of you. If you save me you shall hereafter have success in your undertakings and you shall become a great man."

Then the eagle spoke again, saying, "His words are not true. Turn him away. He can do nothing for you. I, myself will make you great if you will do as I request. It is I who speak the truth. My feet are not held to the earth and I can also fly in the air far above the earth. I am successful in all the things I attempt."

Once more the jack-rabbit made his plea. "Believe him not, and do not turn me away! Even though I must remain upon the ground, and cannot fly like the eagle, still I have knowledge proper to my conditions of life, and I know how to do many things suitably and successfully."

The man made his decision in favor of the jack-rabbit and saved him from the eagle. And the jack-rabbit kept his promise to the man, for he gave him of his own powers and made him successful in his undertakings and helped him with good and wise counsel in times of trouble and doubt and perplexity. So the man gained great renown and honor and influence among his people.

Milton Keynes UK
Ingram Content Group UK Ltd.
UKHW050241220624
444555UK00005BA/472